DEC – – 2014

the WORLD SPLIT OPEN

the WORLD SPLIT OPEN

Great Authors on How and Why We Write

TinHouse Books
Portland, Oregon & Brooklyn, New York

Literary Arts

Portland Arts & Lectures | Writers in the Schools | Oregon Book Awards & Fellowships | Delve

30TH ANNIVERSARY

Published by Tin House Books, Portland, Oregon, and Brooklyn, New York , in collaboration with Literary Arts, Portland, Oregon

Distributed to the trade by Publishers Group West, 1700 Fourth St., Berkeley, CA 94710, www.pgw.com

First US edition 2014
Interior design by Diane Chonette

Printed in the USA
www.tinhouse.com
www.literary-arts.org

CONTENTS

Introduction by Jon Raymond 1

305 Marguerite Cartwright Avenue 5
CHIMAMANDA ADICHIE

Spotty-Handed Villainesses: Problems of Female
Bad Behavior in the Creation of Literature 23
MARGARET ATWOOD

No, But I Saw the Movie 39
RUSSELL BANKS

Childhood of a Writer 57
E. L. DOCTOROW

Finding the Known World 77
EDWARD P. JONES

"Where Do You Get Your Ideas From?" 97
URSULA K. LE GUIN

On "Beauty" 121
MARILYNNE ROBINSON

Fiction to Make Sense of Life 141
WALLACE STEGNER

Morality and Truth in Literature 159
ROBERT STONE

What Is Art For? 173
JEANETTE WINTERSON

CONTRIBUTORS 189
COPYRIGHT NOTES 194

Introduction

JON RAYMOND

Does writing matter?

Let's assume for a second that it doesn't. Writing of the literary variety—poetry, fiction, nonfiction, all of it—persists as a marginal cultural activity, at best. It doesn't generate much in the way of wealth, or almost anything in the way of usable technical knowledge for humankind. Eclipsed long ago by film and television, eclipsed again by interactive gaming technologies, the well-wrought verses, long-form narratives, and digressive essays of quote unquote literature are by now boutique luxury items, spun for elite buyers, going the way of chamber music and the regional ballet company. Mostly it's ladies who dig it.

A basic indifference to serious writing has probably always been the de facto attitude in our culture and has manifested over the years in many forms and with many shadings. There's the bedrock know-nothing-ism of the silent majority who never recovered from the oppression of high school English class; there's the countercultural antielitism that's often just anti-intellectualism in disguise, always ready to dismiss anything a book could teach; there's the idea of good writing as, pace Dick Cheney on the topic of conservationism, a private virtue but not a matter of public concern. Good for you, you're in a book club; I prefer this copy of *Sports Illustrated*. And now, added to the various postures of disregard, is a new typology—the barely covert contempt of our overlords, the engineers of the Internet. The *New York Times* recently profiled a Silicon Valley entrepreneur who had this to say about the secret of his success: "If you can't measure it, you're asking the wrong questions." Such is the metric-based mentality that dominates our world and shapes our postliterary future.

This book is a rebuttal to all that. Literary Arts, an organization founded in 1984, is a bulwark of bookish culture devoted expressly to the proposal that writing does in fact matter. Beginning as a lecture series, in 1993 it joined forces with a sympathetic organization called the Oregon Institute of Literary Arts, founded by Portland lawyer Brian Booth and a group of Oregon writers including Ken Kesey, Ursula K. Le Guin, William Stafford, and Barry Lopez. Together, the fused institutions concurred on a basic, happy mission: namely, to honor and encourage good writing under the presumption that the fruits of the local imagination are a resource on par with Douglas fir trees and marionberries, something to cultivate and protect.

Over the years, Literary Arts has grown into a multipronged nonprofit advocating for writers and writing on numerous fronts. Every year it presents the Oregon Book Awards, an honorific that serves as a main focal point for the local writing community. Every year it delivers fellowships to local writers in the throes of their unfinished work (over $700,000 to over five hundred writers and publishers, as of this writing). It also administrates Writers in the Schools, a residency program placing professional writers in public high school classrooms around the city, as well as organizing teen readings and poetry slams in off-campus locales. And, most famously, it curates Portland Arts and Lectures, bringing some of the world's most notable writers to Portland to share their thoughts before audiences in a gigantic, gilded, Italian rococo revival–style auditorium.

This book is a collection of some of those talks. Does writing matter? Find here if not proof then at least some highly convincing anecdotal evidence in support of the proposition. These essays take for granted that serious writing and serious reading are fundamental to life. They don't constitute a defense of "literature" per se—who'd want to go to the barricades for a word as abstract and high-minded as that?—but instead simply perform the very activity Literary Arts was designed to promote, i.e., the passionate engagement of the human soul with the written word. Open these pages and witness professionals at work. This is how we think clearly. This is how we describe vividly. This is how we moralize deeply. This is how we figure out our politics. This is how we perform all those mental activities that never lose relevance or value, no matter the platform, be it papyrus or a plasma screen.

Some things you have to look forward to in these pages: Wallace Stegner, late in his career, speaking with great honesty and humility about the writing of *Crossing to Safety* and the ongoing adventure of improvising a writing life. Marilynne Robinson, angry and unbowed, preaching with fiery moral clarity on the experience of beauty in contemporary society. Edward P. Jones, on the heels of publishing *The Known World*, waxing wise and self-aware about the wellsprings of his inspiration. Uniting all these writers is a sense of profound modesty in the face of writing's daily difficulty and mystery, and joyful identification as lifelong students of language, history, and human behavior. Over and over again, they genuflect to writing as the visible struggle of humans engaged in moral reflection—indeed, as the very index of consciousness understanding itself. As Robert Stone states, with blazing simplicity: "Storytelling is not a luxury to humanity; it's almost as necessary as bread. We cannot imagine ourselves without it, because the self is a story." Amen.

It's true—the universe would survive without decent writing, much as it did for a trillion or so years before writing was born. And it's true that the vast majority of people on earth will continue to live full, eventful lives without the benefit of Jane Austen or W. S. Merwin. But by this reasoning, you could also argue that almost nothing matters. (Or, rather, you could argue that if you knew how to write well.) People can live without basketball, domestic pets, and real butter, too. If the question is simply one of literal survival in its ultimate sense, eating twigs in the wilderness or Pringles in front of the Xbox, we can survive with almost nothing, we've demonstrated that. For those who want to live in a deeper, funnier, wilder, more troubled, more colorful, more interesting way, a way in which not only writing matters but also beauty, memory, politics, family, and everything else, put on your reading glasses and turn the page. Your people have something to tell you . . .

305 Marguerite Cartwright Avenue

CHIMAMANDA ADICHIE

May 3, 2012

I'd like to start with what I'll call a cultural history of my writing, which is also the story of the house in which I grew up. So I'd like to start by talking about bagels. As a child in Nigeria, I once read an American novel in which a character ate something called a "bagel" for breakfast. I had no idea what a bagel was, but I thought it sounded very elegant, and very exotic. I pronounced it "ba-*gelle*." I desperately wanted to have a ba-*gelle*. My family visited the US for the first time when I was nine, and at the airport in New York, I told my mother that, as a matter of the *gravest* urgency, we had to buy a ba-*gelle*. And so my mother went to a café and bought one. Finally, I would have a ba-*gelle*. Now you can imagine my disappointed surprise when I discovered that this ba-*gelle*, this wonderful, glorious ba-*gelle*, was really just a dense doughnut. I should say I've come to like bagels, but I love to tell this story because I think it illustrates how wonderful books are at enlarging our imaginations. So even though a bagel ended up not being some sort of exquisite confection, the moments in which I thought it was were well worth it, because my imagination soared in delight. And there was also something comforting and instructive in that discovery of a bagel, in the demystifying ordinariness of a bagel—the realization that other people, like me, ate boring food.

As a child, books were the center of my world; stories entranced me, both reading them and writing them. I've been writing since I was old enough to spell. My writing, when it is going well, gives me what I like to describe as "extravagant joy." It is my life's one true passion. It is, in addition to the people I love, what makes me truly happy. And like all real passions, my writing has enormous power over me. There is the extravagant joy when it is going well, and when it is not going well—when I sit in front of my computer and the words simply refuse to come—I feel a soul-crushing anxiety, and I sink into varying levels of depression. Most times, in response to this, I read. I read the authors I love—the poems of Derek Walcott, the prose of John Gregory Brown, the poems of Tanure Ojaide, the prose of Ama Ata Aidoo—and I hope that their words will water my mind, as it were, and get my own words growing again. But if that doesn't work, I take to my bed and eat a lot of ice cream. Or I watch YouTube videos about natural black hair. Or I simply spend all of my time online, shopping—and I particularly favor websites that offer free returns, because I end up returning most of what I buy. But all of this I do with the hope that my words will come back soon, and also with the always hovering fear at the back of my mind that they will not. But so far, the words have always come back.

I write because I have to. I write because I cannot imagine my life without the ability to write, or to imagine, or to dream. I write because I love the solitude of writing, because I love the near-mystical sense of creating characters who sometimes speak to me. I write because I love the possibility of touching another human being with my work, and because I spend a large amount of time in the spaces between the imaginary and the concrete. My writing comes from hope, from melancholy, from rage, and from curiosity. Writing is this wondrous, inexplicable gift that I have been blessed with, but it is also a craft, a steely determination to sit down for hours and write and rewrite until my neck muscles tighten and throb with pain. And then I need a massage.

I have read of some writers' elaborate rituals, and I have also sometimes been tempted to claim an equally elaborate ritual of my own. I've been tempted, for example, to claim that I light red candles, and that I hold incredible yoga positions for hours, or that I recite an Igbo chant and fall into a trance before I actually begin to write. But although my ritual is in truth significantly less colorful than what I would like it to be, it exists, and it involves, among other things, wandering around the house. My husband and I joke about how, when I am at home, and all is quiet, and all distraction turned off, and I am supposed to be writing, I'm instead spending most of the time wandering around the house—from the study, to the bedroom, to the kitchen, and all over again. And my husband will come home from work and say to me, "So how did the wandering go today?" This brings to mind a wonderful quote from Don DeLillo, which goes like this: "Writers go out of their way to secure their solitude. And then, having secured it, they go out of their way to squander it." I feel like Don DeLillo is my kindred spirit. But my wandering, really, is in itself part of the process of trying to get into a creative space. And while I do not light red candles, and there are no particular objects that are central to my creativity, there is a house that is, and that is the house in which I grew up: number 305 Marguerite Cartwright Avenue, at the University of Nigeria, in Nsukka.

Some years ago while I was on book tour, I was asked by an earnest American boy: "Will you always write about Nigeria, or will you write about normal places?" Until then, I had not realized that Nigeria was not normal. I often say that I love Nigeria. Sometimes I'm defensive in professing this love. Yes, there are problems of corruption and inequality, I say, but there's a wonderful proverb from Mali, which says: "Your mother is your mother, even if one of her legs is broken." Of course, this love I profess must be qualified. There is much I do not love about Nigeria, much I wish I could change, much about which I feel by turns anger and shame and bewilderment and disgust. But love is an emotion that does not depend on perfection. And so to say I love Nigeria is to say that I love some kernels of it: my ancestral hometown, Aba; the university primary school—the wonderful, wonderful school where I learned almost everything I know today; and, most of all, the house in which I grew up, number 305 Marguerite Cartwright Avenue.

And so now, a little history. A hundred years ago, West Africa was a diverse, vibrant place. In what is now called Nigeria, there were great kingdoms like the Benin kingdom, the Oyo kingdom; there were small republican groups like the Igbo. Then the Europeans decided that Africa was a rather interesting cake that they wanted to share among themselves, and they met in Berlin and they laid Africa on the table and cut it up like a birthday cake, and one of the slices that went to Britain was in West Africa, and it was a country that they would name after the river Niger: Nigeria. Under British colonialism, Christianity came, and with it Western education. Nigeria had a university college, which was part of the University of London, but shortly before Nigeria became independent in 1960, the government decided that it wanted to establish the first indigenous university, one that would not be affiliated to the University of London, or to any British university. And it chose, for the site of this first university, a town of rolling hills and red dust called Nsukka. A founding committee was set up for the new university, and this committee consisted of Nigerians, British, and Americans. One of the Americans was a woman named Marguerite Cartwright. She was a sociologist and a journalist. When the university was finally started, the first streets on its campus were named after the members of this founding committee. So one of those streets had two-story buildings and large yards and whistling-pine hedges, and it was called Marguerite Cartwright Avenue.

My father was part of the first wave of Nigerian academics who began teaching at Nsukka in 1960. He had a degree in pure and advanced mathematics, but the university already had mathematicians, and so they wanted to start a statistics department, and so my father was hired to teach statistics, even though he really had very little idea what statistics was. And he says that he sometimes just learned as he taught. I wonder how his students are faring now. He lived, at first, in a flat on Elias Avenue. Mr. Elias was a Nigerian member of the founding committee. Then my father married my mother in 1964. He became a senior lecturer and they moved to a new house on Odim Street, into a small bungalow with a tiny veranda and a cluster of flowers by the front door. In 1976, he became a full professor. At this point I think he had gotten the hang of statistics. And because I am a hopeless and utter daddy's girl, I would like to describe my father. He is a quiet, unassuming man. He's a gentle man and a gentleman. He's a committed university teacher; he's a man of immense integrity. And he was also Nigeria's first professor of statistics. I adore him. He turned eighty a few months ago and he still lives in Nsukka. And so when he became a full professor, they moved to another house, a large, spacious bungalow on Mbanefo Street. In September of 1977, after I was born at the university teaching hospital, I was brought back to this house, wrapped in a soft blanket in my mother's arms. I spent the first five years of my life there; I don't remember it very much.

Then, in 1982, my father was appointed deputy vice-chancellor of the university and assigned a new house: number 305 Marguerite Cartwright Avenue. It had a gracious, graveled driveway, a wide yard that in front was bright with red hibiscus and purple bougainvillea, and at the back was dense with avocado, mango, and cashew trees. The first time we saw the house, we looked at the living room, the dining room, the kitchen, and then it was time to go upstairs. I began to cry when I saw the stairs: endless, gleaming a deep burgundy, and insurmountably high. I stood there and refused to climb. Finally my big sister, Uche, held my hand and we took it one step at a time until we got to the top. Only weeks later I was whooping and sliding on a pillow down the banister with my brothers, to see who could do it the fastest before my mother came home.

I remember playing football—I mean what Americans call "soccer"—with my brothers on the lawn outside, and I remember the gardener, whose name was Jumu, asking us not to trample the baby flowers. I remember the frangipani tree that we climbed, and from which I once fell, and the guava tree, to which we tied chickens before they were killed for Sunday lunch. I remember riding bicycles up and down the slope of Marguerite Cartwright Avenue. I remember the horridly flat, oversize cockroaches that crawled in with the rainy season and smelled like something rotten. We called them "American cockroaches." They were not the usual small size of Nigerian cockroaches, and I'm not sure whether they were called American cockroaches because they were larger than normal, but I think the story was that they were not indigenous to

Nigeria and that they had been brought by one of the American staff of the university.

My brother Okey, a keen animal lover, had a collection of rabbits, guinea pigs, and turtles. He kept them in the back, which was also where our house help lived and where we roasted cashew nuts. A rickety shed made of corrugated iron stood at the entrance to the compound, a booth for the security guards—old men in brown uniforms and matching berets who often slept through hot afternoons. I would come to know one of them well, the gentle, ashy-skinned Vincent, who would ask my brothers and me to sit beside him in the shed and would tell us Igbo folk stories about the cunning tortoise. I shared the biggest room upstairs with my brothers Okey and Kene. It had three beds, dressers, a wardrobe. It did not have a desk. It led out to a veranda where we played, where I read Enid Blyton, where I skulked and watched the older, handsome boy from next door. The veranda had a second door that led to the study, my father's dusty lair, lined with shelves of statistics journals and dominated by a large desk on which were placed files, books, paper clips, pens, and, at the farthest corner, the black rotary phone. I wonder now why the phone was kept in the study instead of the corridor downstairs, but it was, and so throughout secondary school I had uncomfortable conversations with friends while my father sat there, marking his students' papers. Parts of the desk were so dusty, I wrote down phone numbers with my finger, or I just doodled. I wrote my first book, at ten, at that desk, in a lined exercise notebook; it was titled *Down Macintosh Lane*.

Before we moved into number 305 Marguerite Cartwright Avenue, Chinua Achebe and his family lived there. I realize now what an interesting coincidence it is, that I grew up in a house previously occupied by the writer whose work is most important to me. There must have been literary spirits in the bathroom upstairs, and I say this because I often got story ideas after I had bucket baths in that bathroom. But the only manifest Achebe legacy was on a window ledge in the dining room, scratch-written in the childish hand of his daughter—her name, Nwando Achebe. I did not find it particularly remarkable at the time that I lived in this house. The university campus was a small place; people moved in and out of university housing; the academic community was a small one. Years later, when my first novel was published, I told my editor, "You know, it's kind of interesting—I lived in the house previously occupied by Chinua Achebe." I said it as sort of a passing comment, and she stopped and stared at me and she said, "What? This is the most interesting thing you've told me about yourself."

So now two little stories about Achebe's *Things Fall Apart*: I read a lot of British children's literature when I was growing up, and I was particularly enamored of Enid Blyton. I think Enid Blyton must be turning over and over in her grave because I talk about her all the time. And so I thought that books had to have white people in them, by their very nature. When I started to write, as soon as I was old enough to spell, I wrote the kinds of stories that I was reading. I had all of these characters who were white, and who lived on Macintosh Lane, and who had dogs called "Socks," which was an improbable name for a dog in Nigeria. And also my characters drank a lot of ginger beer, because Blyton's characters spent a lot of time drinking ginger beer, never mind that I had no idea what ginger beer was. And for many years afterward I would have this intense desire for ginger beer, but that's another story. And then I read Achebe's *Things Fall Apart*, and I like to describe it as a glorious shock of discovery. Here were characters who had Igbo names, and who ate yams, and who inhabited a world that was similar to mine. His novel taught me that my world was worthy of literature, that books could also be about people like me. It was about the same time that I read Camara Laye's novel *The African Child*, a beautiful, beautiful book that is elegiac and wonderfully defensive, and that also made me think of my world as worthy of literature. But I like to think of Chinua Achebe as the writer who gave me permission to write my stories. Although his characters were familiar in many ways, their world was also incredibly exotic in other ways, because they lived without the things that I saw as the norm in my life. They did not have cars, or electricity, or phones. They did not eat fried rice. In fact, I was horrified that they had *fufu* for breakfast, because I consider *fufu* too heavy for breakfast. In other words, they lived the life that my great-grandfather might have lived.

And this brings me to my second *Things Fall Apart* story. I came to the US to go to school because I was fleeing the study of medicine. When you do well in school in Nigeria, you're expected to become what we call "a professional," which really means a doctor. An engineer if you're a boy, or maybe a lawyer. So I was expected to become a doctor, and I had been in what was called a "science track" in secondary school, which means that I had done the chemistries and the physics and the biologies, because that's what you did if you did well in school. And then I started the college of medicine, and after a year I realized that I would be a very unhappy doctor. And so, to prevent the future inadvertent deaths of patients, I fled. And America was my escape. But before I arrived in Philadelphia, my friend Ada, who was also Nigerian but who had been in the US for a number of years, found me a room in a four-bedroom apartment that I would share with some American students. I remember how surprised my roommates were to see me. They said I was wearing "American clothes," by which they meant the pair of jeans I had bought at the market in Nsukka. And then I realized that maybe *Things Fall Apart* had played a role in this. They might have read it in high school, but maybe their teacher forgot to tell them that it was set in the Nigeria of a hundred years ago.

But back to number 305 Marguerite Cartwright Avenue. The campus of the University of Nigeria was a small, safe, and happy place. Everybody knew everybody else; the children of the staff all attended the staff primary school, and all went to the staff children's library, and so in that house, number 305 Marguerite Cartwright Avenue, I began to write. I wrote at the dining table when I could not use the study desk because my father was working or because a sibling was on the phone. The dining table was light green and long, and it was the family dumping ground of newspapers, university circulars, wedding invitations, magazines, bananas, ground nuts—and the tiny ants that lived underneath it appeared after breakfast to crowd around bits of sugar or bread. I always cleared a space for myself at one end, opposite the grand old wood-paneled air conditioner, which was used so rarely that a puff of dust always burst out first, before cool air followed. I remember that we seemed to put it on only during birthday parties. And it was noisy—it made a loud whooshing sound—and so, during birthday parties when the living room was full of friends, there was always that loud sound of the air conditioner in the background.

Okey and Kene and I had separate bedrooms after our older siblings left home. Mine had a girlish table where I displayed my lotions, my creams, my powder compacts. It still did not have a desk. In 1997 I left home, and when I returned four years later with the final page proofs of my first novel, my parents had put a writing desk in my room. It was square and sturdy, and I spread out my page proofs and edited them there. A few years later, when I was writing my second novel, *Half of a Yellow Sun*, which is set during the Nigeria-Biafra War, I knew I needed to write a large part of it in Nigeria. I needed to go to my ancestral hometown; I needed to smell the dust there. And I also needed to be in number 305 Marguerite Cartwright, that house that had nurtured me, where I believed the literary spirits still hovered. When I returned, my parents had installed an air conditioner in my room. It was more modern, less noisy, and the lights blinked when I turned it on. I transcribed interviews at the dining table or at my father's desk in the study, but I wrote only in my room, and from time to time I would look out at the veranda, which was no longer used much. Years of rain had stained the floor a dull gray. And I finished my novel there, sitting in my room and looking out at the veranda that had witnessed my childhood.

I have often been asked why I chose to write about Biafra, and I like to say that I did not choose Biafra, but it chose me. I cannot honestly intellectualize my interest in the war; it is a subject I have known for very long that I would write about. I was born seven years after the Nigeria-Biafra War ended, and yet the war is not mere history for me. It is also memory. I grew up in the shadow of Biafra. I knew vaguely about the war as a child—that my grandfathers had died, that my parents had lost everything they owned. But long before my parents—particularly my father—began to talk under my keen questioning about their specific experiences, I was very much aware of how this war had haunted my family, how it colored the paths our lives had taken. My paternal grandfather died more than a year before the war ended. Because he was in Biafra I, and my father was in a region called Biafra II, and they were separated by an occupied road, my father could not go to the refugee camp where his father was buried. My father is the first son, and he takes his first-son responsibilities very seriously. In Igbo culture, one of the responsibilities of the first son is to ensure that his father gets a proper funeral. And so it broke my father's heart that his father died and he couldn't even go to see where he was buried. When the war ended in 1970, the first thing he wanted to do was to go and see where his father was buried. He went to the refugee camp, which used to be a secondary school before the war, and asked where the grave was, and somebody pointed to this vague expanse and said, "We buried the people there." It was a mass grave. My father, who is the most undramatic of people, bent down and took a handful of sand, and he has kept the sand ever since.

My mother has still not spoken very much about losing her father, also in a refugee camp, but she has spoken about the other things she lost—her wig, her china that she had brought back from London. She has spoken about going from making toast and scrambled eggs for her two little daughters to standing in line and fighting for dried egg yolk from the relief center. I am still known to cry stupidly about some of these stories, about the tiny losses that so many people endured, about this trail of physical and metaphysical losses. But I wanted to write a novel. I wanted to write about what I like to call the "grittiness" of being human. I wanted to write a book about relationships, about people who have sex, and eat food, and laugh. Because in addition to those terrible stories about the war, I also heard stories about weddings, about people falling in love. I was concerned with certain questions about what it means to be human. When you are deprived of the comforts of the life you know, when you go from eating sandwiches to eating rats, how does it change your relationship with yourself, with the people you love?

After the novel was published, I was stunned by how many people embraced it as their own personal story. At my readings, particularly in Nigeria, women would start to cry, and say, "Thank you for writing this, because finally I can tell my family what I went through." Men would get choked up talking about how they had been conscripted in the war as boys, and young people of my generation would get emotional talking about how they finally understood their parents, or how they finally understood our history as Nigerians. The novel started a conversation about a part of our history that remains contested and contentious. It humbled me and it made me very happy.

There is much that I cannot explain about my writing process. I find it difficult, for example, to answer what I think is the laziest question that anyone can ask a writer: Where do you get your inspiration? The question itself assumes that inspiration can somehow be explained and packaged into logical and digestible bits. But anything can be a source of inspiration. I'm a keen watcher of people, for example, and I carry with me a notebook to record whatever strikes me: the color of a woman's lipstick, an overheard conversation between strangers in a café, the slump of a man's shoulders in the departure lounge of an airport—all of which may become part of a piece of fiction. To write realistic fiction as I do, is, I think, to try and make sense of the world by storytelling, by streamlining the chaotic nature of life into some sort of narrative with emotive points, and hopefully by doing that, we remind ourselves what it means to be human. The process is a mix of the conscious and the unconscious—I'm not always in control of what I write. And for me, one of the magical things about writing fiction is that you start a story and you are in control and then sometimes the story just overtakes you and characters do things that surprise you. But when I tell my brothers this, that sometimes a character did something, my brothers look at me as though I'm just a little crazy and they say, "What do you mean? You wrote the book. What do you mean, the characters *did* something?" It's the sort of thing that's difficult for people who don't write to understand.

My first novel, *Purple Hibiscus*, came organically—and the story more or less wrote itself—but it helped that I was miserable. In the middle of a freezing Connecticut winter, I was homesick for the warmth of Nsukka. I was thrilled that somebody actually wanted to publish the book, and I thought that maybe three people would buy it—my sister, my brother, and my best friend. And I was wonderfully surprised when more than three people bought it. But I also quickly realized that to be a Nigerian and an African, and to be published outside of home, was often to have my work looked at through a political lens. I would do readings outside of the continent of Africa and often be asked—or even be told—that my novel was a political allegory, that my abusive father character represented Nigeria's brutal dictator. Which was news to me.

I sometimes wondered why nobody asked me about love and about personal motivations and why I constantly had to be asked about the sociopolitical. Of course I know the reason: so little is known about the part of the world from which I come that it is not very surprising that a novel would be seen as some kind of native explanation. But it does not change the truth, which is that when I sat down to write that father character in *Purple Hibiscus*, I was not thinking, "I shall now write an important allegorical representation of Nigeria's military culture." I just wanted to write a human story about a man who was struggling with his demons.

I think there are two ways to think about fiction: as a critic and as a creative person, and my general rule is to think as a critic only about the work of other people, never about my own work, otherwise I will in fact start writing a novel with the idea of writing "an important allegorical representation of Nigeria's military culture." But knowing that so little is known about Nigeria and, by extension, Africa, makes me a little wary of writing truthfully about what interests me.

My best friend, Uju, complains—and she's been complaining the past few months, because I have been immersed in writing, in trying to finish a new novel—that she never sees me, and I never return calls, and we don't spend as much time together as we should. And this is true, because when my writing is going well, I become very inward. I lock myself up for weeks, and sometimes I don't shower—not that you need to have that too-much-information bit—and it makes me think about the sacrifices that come with writing: the calls that are not returned, the time that you haven't spent with the people you love, because for me love means time spent. And this often leaves me with a clutch of small regrets in my soul. But it's a sacrifice I make willingly; it's a choice I make for my writing. And so my best friend, in her complaining, said to me, "Well, just kill the character already so we can hang out!" And I said, "What are you talking about?" And she said, "Well, in your writing somebody always has to die." And I wasn't quite sure how to take that—I was quite taken aback, actually—and then I thought about it for a while, and I realized, you know, she is right. People don't always die in my work, but in a larger sense, as a writer and also as a reader, I'm drawn to what is dark; I am drawn to melancholy; a kind of beautiful sadness is what I find most moving in writing and reading fiction.

My brother has a son who's very bright but who doesn't like to read, and so my brother said to me, "Why don't you consider writing for children? Maybe this will make Chinadun read." I thought about it for a while and then I thought, "You know, I really love children; I don't want to be responsible for their being traumatized." So I thought, "No, I won't write children's books, I don't think that's a good idea." And so I write about love and the possibility of connection and all of that, but in the end my artistic vision is largely a dark one. And I sometimes wonder whether being African means that I must always indulge in these fragile negotiations in order to explore my artistic vision fully. When I write about war, for example, I find myself thinking, "Does this only perpetuate the stereotype of Africa as a place of war?" So far I have kept from making artistic choices based on this, but I do think about it, and it brings a certain discomfort.

I will never forget how moved I was to read some years ago Nelson Mandela's description of Chinua Achebe's *Things Fall Apart*. He called it "the book in whose presence the prison walls came down." And I have a much smaller, but similar personal story. Last year, I was reading a piece in the *New York Times* about an American woman called Lori Berenson who had been convicted in Peru for aiding a leftist group, and she had been sentenced to twenty years in prison. She'd been granted parole, and her mother gave an interview in which she talked about how her daughter had coped during her years in captivity. Reading, not surprisingly, was central to her coping. And then I read a line where her mother said that one of the books that was a favorite was a book called *Half of a Yellow Sun*. At first I read past; I thought, "No, it can't be my book"—it just seemed so improbable—and then the book was described as a book set in Nigeria, and I thought, "Wait, it *is* my book!" Now here was a woman I did not know of, who was not Nigerian, who was not in any way connected to Biafra, and yet this book had been meaningful to her at a very difficult time in her life. And reading that, I felt so moved, and I remember thinking, "Fiction *does* matter."

When I first came to the US, American fiction was very important to me. Even though I had consumed a lot of American media, as most of the world does; even though, growing up in Nsukka, I had watched *Sesame Street* and I was very familiar with Big Bird and Elmo, I felt a sense of dislocation when I arrived. I thought that every black family would be like *The Cosby Show*. You can imagine my surprise when I discovered that this was not so. And so I started to read American fiction. I read Toni Morrison, James Baldwin, Philip Roth, John Steinbeck, Willa Cather, John Updike, and Mary Gaitskill. I read everything I could find. And in a way, America started to make sense to me.

So now, to end the story about number 305 Marguerite Cartwright Avenue: four years ago, my parents moved out of the house. They're now retired from the university, and the house has been assigned to another family. I was in the US when they moved out of the house, and so the week that they moved out, I talked to them on the phone and I asked them ridiculous questions: "Did you find that doll that I lost in primary school?" "Did you keep my secondary-school textbooks?" And throughout the conversation I fought tears. My parents talked about the cartons they had bought and the lorries they had hired. They sounded practical and calm. "How could they not see how momentous this was?" I thought. "We're leaving behind twenty-five years of our lives." But of course they did; they simply are not much given to melodrama, as I am. I hung up that day after talking to my parents, and I thought about the last time that I was in the house. There was a power failure at night, and in the pitch-blackness I walked from my room, down the stairs, and into the dining room to find the candle in the cabinet. And I did not stumble once.

Spotty-Handed Villainesses: Problems of Female Bad Behavior in the Creation of Literature

MARGARET ATWOOD

February 2, 1994

I've recently developed the sneaking suspicion that writers should not give lectures, not just because they're too much like homework to prepare, but also because writers don't really have a field of expertise, apart of course from their tricks of craft, which they are usually unwilling to discuss. In saying they don't really have a field of expertise I'm not downgrading them, merely pointing out the obvious. Writers, particularly novelists, are among the last great generalists. If I were a dentist addressing fellow dentists, or a plumber among plumbers, you would perhaps learn something of use. As it is, what can I possibly have to say that you don't already secretly know? But being a writer—and although some of the patron gods of writers are the dignified and beautiful muses, another one is the dishonest Mercury, god of tricksters and thieves—I frequently engage, at least imaginatively, in pursuits of which I disapprove. So here I am giving, if not a lecture, at least something that might pass as one, if you squint.

My title is: "Spotty-Handed Villainesses." My subtitle is: "Problems of Female Bad Behavior in the Creation of Literature." I should probably have said, "in the creation of novels," because it's my novelist's outfit I'm wearing at the moment. Female bad behavior may occur in lyric poems, of course, but not at very great length. Somebody has asked whether the spotty-handedness in my title referred to age spots. Was my lecture perhaps going to send her on that once-forbidden but now red-hot topic, the menopause, without which any collection of female-obilia would be incomplete? I hasten to point out that my title is not age related. It refers neither to age spots nor to youth spots, once known as "zits." Instead it recalls that most famous of spots, the invisible but indelible one on the hand of wicked Lady Macbeth. "Spot" as in guilt, "spot" as in blood, "spot" as in "Out, damned." Lady Macbeth was spotted, Ophelia unspotted. Both came to sticky ends, but there's a world of difference.

I'll get around to the spotty women in good time. But first let me go over some essentials, which may be insulting to your intelligence but which are comforting to mine, because they help me to keep my mind on what I'm supposed to be doing. If I may appear to be flogging a few dead horses, horses that have been put out of their pain long ago in some happy but sequestered circles, let me assure you that this is because the horses are not in fact dead, but are out there in the world, galloping around as vigorously as ever. How do I know this? I read my mail. Also, on occasion, I listen to the questions that people ask me, both in interviews and during the question-and-answer periods after public readings. The kinds of questions I'm talking about have to do with what a writer should be doing, and how the characters in a novel ought to behave. There is a widespread tendency to judge such characters as if they were job applicants or public servants or prospective roommates or somebody you're considering marrying. Let me underline the fact that the characters in novels are none of the above, and if they were, we would all be in deep trouble. What are they, then, and how should we go about responding to them? Or, from my side of the page, which is blank when I begin, how should I go about creating them? Which raises the further question: What is a novel, anyway? Only a very foolish person would attempt to give a definitive answer to that, beyond stating the more-or-less-obvious fact that it is a prose narrative of some length that purports on the reverse of the title page not to be true but seeks nevertheless to convince its readers that it is. As I said, Mercury is one of its patrons, and all writers are, among other things, con artists.

But sometimes, when I find myself among readers; that is, among the trusting, I get confused, as I discover that such people are not treating me with the suspicion that I deserve. They are not hiding the silverware and disbelieving my claim that I'm actually the telephone repairperson, as they ought to do. Instead they invite me with great kindliness into their living rooms and expect me to act as some sort of cross between an old-time circuit rider and an astrologer and to solve their life problems for them. We con artists do tell the truth in a way, but as Emily Dickinson said, we "tell it slant." By indirection we find direction out.

So here, for easy reference, is an elimination dance list of what novels are not:

A novel is not a sociological textbook, although its true-to-life details must convince. If there's a brand of oven cleaner in it, that brand should actually have existed at the time. The toads in its imaginary garden must be real toads, but the garden is an imaginary one for all that. This is not, by the way, an argument for old-time realism, which leaves too much out.

Nor is a novel a political tract, although politics, in the sense of human power structures, are germane to it. If its main design on us is to convert us to something—whether that something be Christianity, capitalism, a belief in marriage as the only answer to a maiden's prayer, or feminism—we are likely to sniff it out and rebel. As André Gide once remarked, "It is with noble sentiments that bad literature gets written." This is not to say that "politics," in quotation marks, cannot form the substance of a novel. One of my own most favorite nineteenth-century novels is Zola's *Germinal*; another is George Eliot's *Middlemarch*. Both are highly political in an obvious way. But yet another is *Wuthering Heights*, which does not have any overt politics in it at all, though it could be read as a piece of subversion through and through. As I've said, novelists are a devious bunch.

A novel is not a how-to book; it will not show you how to conduct a successful life, although some novels may be read this way. Is *Pride and Prejudice* about how a sensible middle-class nineteenth-century woman can snare an appropriate man with a good income, which is the best she can hope for out of life given the limitations of her situation? Partly. But not completely.

A novel is not a moral tract. Its characters are not all models of good behavior; or, if they are, we probably won't read it. A novel is, however, inexorably linked with notions of morality, because it is about human beings, and human beings divide behavior into good and bad. The characters in a novel judge each other, and the reader judges the characters. However, the success of a novel does not depend on a not-guilty verdict from the reader. As Keats said,

Shakespeare took as much delight in creating an Iago, that archvillain, as he did in creating the virtuous Imogen. I would say, probably more—and the proof of it is that I'd wager money you're more likely to know which play Iago is in.

But although a novel is not a political tract, a how-to book, a sociology textbook, or a pattern of correct morality, it is also not merely a beautiful structure, a piece of art for art's sake, divorced from real life in its considerations, whether social or psychological. It cannot do without a conception of form—and a structure, true—but its roots are in the mud. It may put out lovely, lyrical flowers, certainly, but such flowers are built up out of the rawness of its raw materials. Novels are made of language, and language, being human, is messy. In short, the novel is ambiguous and multifaceted, not because it is perverse, although it may be that as well, but because it attempts to grapple with what was once referred to as "the human condition," and it does so using a medium that is as slippery as a greased lawyer, as stretchy as an old-time panty girdle, and as hard to pin down as a bowl of Jell-O—namely, the language itself.

Let me share with you some of the problems that beset the practicing novelist. Let us say the practicing *female* novelist, although what follows can be extended to the more innocent sex as well. Literary critics start, usually, with a text. They then address questions to this text, which they attempt to answer, "What does it mean?" being both the most basic and the most difficult. Novelists, on the other hand, start with the blank page, to which they similarly address questions. But the questions are different. Instead of asking, "What does it mean?" they ask, "Is this the right word, the right sentence, the right paragraph?" The critic asks, "What's happening?" The novelist, "What happens next?" The critic asks, "What kind of story is this?" The novelist, "What kind of story should this be?" The critic asks, "Is this believable?" The novelist, "How can I get them to believe this?" The novelist, echoing Marshall McLuhan's famous dictum that art is what you can get away with, says, "How can I pull it off?" as if the novel itself were a kind of bank robbery, whereas the critic is all too often liable to exclaim, in the mode of the policeman making the arrest, "Aha! You can't get away with that!"

In short, the novelist has to contend with the following questions: What kind of story shall I choose to tell? Is it, for instance, comic or tragic or melodramatic or all? How shall I tell it? Who will be at the center of it, and will this person be a) admirable or b) not? And, more important than it may sound, will it have a happy ending or not? No matter what you are writing, what genre and in what style, whether cheap formula or high-minded experiment, you will still have to answer, in the course of your writing, these essential questions. And unless you solve the problem of how to interest the reader—at least a few readers—you won't have any.

What this means in actual fact is that any story you tell must have a conflict of some sort, and it must have suspense. This sounds like Film Writing 101, but it is nevertheless true. Let's put a woman at the center of the story and see what happens, keeping in mind that art is what you can get away with—that is, you have to suck the reader in—and that conflict and suspense are necessary. Now there is a whole new set of questions: Will the conflict be supplied by the natural world? Is our protagonist lost in the jungle, caught in a hurricane, or pursued by sharks? If so, the story will be an adventure story, and her job is to run away—or else to combat the snakes or whatever, displaying courage and fortitude, or else cowardice and stupidity. If there is a man in the story as well, the plot will alter in other directions. He will be a rescuer, an enemy, a companion in struggle, a sex bomb, or someone rescued by the woman. Once upon a time, the first would have been more probable, that is, more believable to the reader, but times have changed, art is what you can get away with, and the other possibilities have now entered the picture.

Stories about space invasions are similar, in that the threat comes from outside and the goal for the character, whether achieved or not, is survival. War stories per se, ditto, in that the main threat is external. Vampire and werewolf stories are more complicated, as are ghost stories. In these, the threat is from outside, true, but the threatening thing may also conceal a split-off part of the character's own psyche. Henry James's *The Turn of the Screw* and Bram Stoker's *Dracula* are in large part animated by such hidden agendas, and both revolve around notions of female sexuality. Once, all werewolves were male, and female vampires, with the exception of Sheridan Le Fanu's *Carmilla*, were mere sidekicks to the male vampire. But there are now female werewolves, and women are moving in on the star bloodsucking roles too. Whether this is good or bad news, I hesitate to say.

Detective and espionage stories may combine many elements but would not be what they are without a crime, a criminal, a tracking down, and a revelation at the end. Again, all sleuths were once male, but sleuthesses are now prominent, for which I hope they lay a votive ball of wool from time to time upon the tomb of the sainted Miss Marple. We live in an age not only of gender crossover but also of genre crossover, so you can throw all of the above into the cauldron and stir.

Then there are stories classed as "serious literature," which center not on external threats, although some of these may exist, but on relationships among the characters. This is where the questions really get difficult. As I've said, the novel has its roots in the mud, and part of the mud is history. And part of the history we've had recently is the history of the women's movement, and the women's movement has influenced how people read, and therefore what you can get away with in art. Some of this influence has been beneficial: for instance, whole areas of life that were once considered nonliterary or subliterary, such as the problematical nature of homemaking, the hidden depths of motherhood and of daughterhood, the once-forbidden realms of incest and child abuse, have been brought inside the circle that demarcates the writable from the nonwritable. Other things, such as the Cinderella ending—girl marries Prince Charming and lives happily ever after—have been called into question. As one lesbian writer remarked to me, the only happy ending she found believable anymore was the one in which girl meets girl and ends up with girl. But that was fifteen years ago, and the bloom is off even that romantic rose.

To keep you from being too depressed, let me emphasize yet once again that none of this means that you, personally, cannot find happiness with a good man, a good woman, or a good pet canary—just as the creation of a bad female character doesn't mean that women should lose the vote. If bad male characters in novels meant that for men, all men would be disenfranchised immediately. We are talking about what you can get away with in art—that is, what you can make believable. When Shakespeare wrote his sonnets to his dark-haired mistress, he wasn't saying that blondes were ugly; he was just pushing against the notion that only blondes were beautiful. The tendency of experimental literature is to include the hitherto excluded, which often has the effect of rendering ludicrous the conventions that have just preceded the innovation.

So the form of the ending, whether happy or not, does not have to do with how people live their lives. There is a great deal of variety in that department; and, after all, in life everything ends with death, which is not true of the novel. Instead, it has something to do with what literary conventions the writer is following or pulling apart at the moment. Happy endings of the "Cinderella" kind do exist in books, of course, but they have been relegated largely to genre fiction, such as Harlequin romances.

To summarize some of the literary benefits of the women's movement: more inclusion; the expansion of the parameters available to writers, both in character and in language; a sharp-eyed examination of the way power works in gender relations; and the exposure of much of this as socially constructed—a vigorous exploration of many hitherto mysterious territories of experience. But as with any political movement that comes out of real oppression—I emphasize here *real* oppression—there was also, in the first decade, at least, of the present movement, a tendency to polarize morality by gender. That is, women were intrinsically good, and men bad. To divide along allegiance lines, that is: women who slept with men were sleeping with the enemy; women who wore high heels and makeup were instantly suspect; defects in women were ascribable to the patriarchal system and would cure themselves once that system was abolished; and so forth.

Such polarizations may be necessary to some phases of political movements, but they are usually problematical for novelists. If a novelist writing at that time was also a feminist, she found her choices self-restricted, or at least rendered more difficult. Were all heroines to be essentially spotless of soul, struggling against, fleeing from, or done in by male oppression? Was the only plot to be *The Perils of Pauline*, with a myriad of mustache-twirling villains but minus the rescuing hero? Did suffering prove you were good? If so—think hard about this—wasn't it all for the best that women did so much of it? Did we face a situation in which women could do no wrong but could only have wrong done to them? Wasn't that just falling into the trap represented by the old children's rhyme about girls and boys, in which girls are made of sugar and spice, and all things nice, and boys of snaps and snails and puppy dogs' tails (excuse the phallic symbolism)? Were women being condemned yet again to that alabaster pedestal so beloved of the Victorian age, when woman as better than man gave men a license to be gleefully and enjoyably worse than women, while all the while proclaiming that they couldn't help it because it was their nature? Women were condemned to virtue for life, slaves in the salt mines of goodness. How intolerable.

Of course, the feminist analysis made some kinds of behavior available to female characters, which, under the old dispensation—the prefeminist one—would have been considered bad, but under the new one were praiseworthy. A female character could rebel against social strictures, sexually and in other ways, without then having to throw herself in front of a train. She could think the unthinkable and say the unsayable; she could flout authority; she could feel and express pain and anger. She could do new, bad/good things, such as leaving her husband and even deserting her children and living with another woman. Such activities and emotions, however, were, according to the new moral thermometer of the times, not really bad at all. They were good, and the women who did them were praiseworthy. I'm not against such plots; I just don't think they are the only ones.

And there were certain new no-no's. For instance, was it at all permissible anymore to talk about women's will to power, because weren't women supposed, by nature, to be communal egalitarians? Could one depict the scurvy behavior often practiced by women against one another, or by little girls against other little girls? Could one examine the seven deadly sins in their female versions—to remind you: pride, anger, lust, envy, avarice, greed, and sloth—without being considered antifeminist? Or was a mere mention of such things—although we all knew they existed—tantamount to aiding and abetting the enemy, namely the male power structure? Were we to have a warning hand clapped over our mouths yet once again, to prevent us from saying the unsayable, although the unsayable had changed? Were we to listen to our mothers, yet once again, as they intoned, "If you can't say anything nice, don't say anything at all"? Hadn't men been giving women a bad rap for centuries? Shouldn't we form a kind of wall of silence around the badness of women, or at best explain it away by saying it was the fault of Big Daddy or, permissible too, it seems, of Big Mom? Big Mom, that agent of the patriarchy, that pro-natalist, got it in the neck from certain 1970s feminists, though mothers were admitted into the fold again once some of these women turned into them. In a word, were women to be homogenized—one woman is the same as the other—and deprived of free will, as in, "The patriarchy made her do it"? Or in another word, were men to get all the juicy parts?

Literature cannot do without bad behavior, as you will discover after one minute of reflection or a reading of Samuel Richardson's supremely boring goodness novel, *Sir Charles Grandison*. But was all the bad behavior to be reserved for men? Was it to be all Iago and Mephistopheles, and were Jezebel and Medea and Delilah and Regan and Goneril and spotty-handed Lady Macbeth and Rider Haggard's powerful superfemme fatale in *She* to be banished from view? I hope not. Women characters arise; take back the night. In particular, take back the Queen of the Night. It's a great part, and due for revision.

To share with you again: I've always known that there were some spellbinding, evil parts for women. For one thing, I was taken at the age of five to see *Snow White and the Seven Dwarfs*. Never mind the Protestant work ethic of the dwarfs. Never mind the tedious housework as virtuous motif. Never mind the fact that Snow White is a vampire. (Anyone who lies in a glass coffin without decaying and then comes to life again must be.) The truth is that I was paralyzed by the scene in which the evil queen drinks the magic potion and changes her shape. What power; what untold possibilities!

Also, I was exposed to the complete, unexpurgated *Grimm's Fairy Tales* at an impressionable age. Fairy tales have had a bad reputation among feminists for a while, partly because they'd been cleaned up on the erroneous supposition that little children don't like gruesome gore, and partly because they'd been selected to fit the 1950s "Prince Charming is your goal" ethos. So "Cinderella" and "The Sleeping Beauty" were okay, though "The Youth Who Set Out to Learn What Fear Was"—which featured a good many rotting corpses, plus a woman who was smarter than her husband—was not. But many of these tales were originally told and retold by women, and these unknown women left their mark. There's a wide range of heroines in these tales. Passive good girls, yes, but adventurous, resourceful women as well, and proud ones, slothful ones, foolish ones, envious and greedy ones, and also many wise women, and a variety of evil witches—both in disguise and not—and bad stepmothers, and wicked, ugly sisters, and false brides as well. The stories, and the figures themselves, have immense vitality, partly because no punches are pulled—in the versions I read, the barrels of nails and the red-hot shoes were left intact—and because no emotion is unrepresented. Singly, the female characters are limited and two-dimensional, but put all together, they form a rich, five-dimensional picture.

Female characters who behave badly can of course be used as sticks to beat women, though so can female characters who behave well. Witness the cult of the Virgin Mary—better than you'll ever be. And the legends of the female saints and martyrs—just cut on the dotted line, and, minus one body part, there's your saint. And the only really good woman is a dead woman, so if you're so good, why aren't you dead? Women were once provided with numerous cautionary tales featuring bad behavior, followed by gruesome ends, as a warning to us to stay indoors and keep our noses, etcetera, clean.

But female bad characters can also act as keys to doors we need to open, and as mirrors in which we can see more than just a pretty face. They can be explorations of moral freedom, because everyone's choices are limited and women's choices have been more limited than men's—but that doesn't mean women can't make choices. Such characters can pose the question of responsibility, because if you want power, you have to accept responsibility, and actions produce consequences. I'm not suggesting an agenda here, just some possibilities. Nor am I prescribing—just wondering. If there's a closed-off road, the curious speculate about why it's closed off and where it might lead if followed, and evil women have been, for a while recently, a somewhat closed-off road—at least for fiction writers.

While I was writing this, I thought back over some bad female literary characters—not all written by women, it's true, but available to women now, because if a character has been written, she can always be rewritten. Witness Rochester's mad wife in *Jane Eyre*, rewritten by Jean Rhys in *Wide Sargasso Sea*. If you were doing this on a blackboard, you might set up a kind of grid: Bad Women Who Do Bad Things for Bad Reasons; Good Women Who Do Good Things for Good Reasons; Good Women Who Do Bad Things for Good Reasons; Bad Women Who Do Bad Things for Good Reasons; and so forth. But a grid would just be a beginning, because there are so many factors involved.

For instance: what the character thinks is bad, what the reader thinks is bad, and what the author thinks is bad may all be different. Also, motivations, actions, and consequences may be quite separate.

But let me define a thoroughly evil person as one who intends to do evil, and for purely selfish reasons. The queen in "Snow White" would fit that. So would Regan and Goneril, Lear's evil daughters. Very little can be said in their defense, except that they seem to have been against the patriarchy. Lady Macbeth, however, did her wicked murder for a conventionally acceptable reason, one that would win approval for her in corporate business circles: she was furthering her husband's career. She pays the corporate wife price, too—she subdues her own nature and has a nervous breakdown as a result. Similarly, Jezebel was merely trying to please a sulky husband; he refused to eat his dinner until he got hold of Naboth's vineyard, so Jezebel had its owner bumped off. Wifely devotion, as I say. The amount of sexual baggage that has accumulated around this figure is astounding, since she doesn't do anything remotely sexual in the original story except put on lipstick.

The story of Medea—whose husband, Jason, married a new princess and who then poisoned the bride and murdered her own two children—has been interpreted in various ways. In some versions, Medea is a witch and commits infanticide out of revenge, but the play by Euripedes is surprisingly neo-feminist. There's quite a lot about how tough it is to be a woman, and Medea's motivation is commendable: she doesn't want her children to fall into hostile hands and be cruelly abused, which is also the situation of the child-killing mother in Toni Morrison's *Beloved*. A good woman, then, who does a bad thing for a good reason. Hardy's Tess of the D'Urbervilles kills her nasty lover due to sexual complications. Here too we are in the realm of female as victim, doing a bad thing for a good reason, which, I suppose, places such stories right beside the front page, along with women who kill their abusive husbands. According to a recent *New York Times* story, the average jail sentence in the United States for men who kill their wives is four years, but for women who kill their husbands, no matter what the provocation, it's twenty. For those who think equality is already with us, I leave the statistics to speak for themselves.

These women characters are all murderers. Then there are the seducers. Here again, the motive varies. I have to say too that with the change in sexual mores, the mere seduction of a man no longer rates too high on the sin scale. But try asking a number of women what the worst thing is that another woman could possibly do to them   chances are, the answer will involve the theft of a sexual partner. Some famous seductresses have really been patriotic espionage agents—Delilah, for instance, was an early Mata Hari, working for the Philistines, trading sex for military information. Judith, who seduced the enemy general, Holofernes, and then cut off his head and brought it home in a sack, was treated as a heroine, although she has troubled men's imaginations through the centuries. Witness the number of male painters who have depicted her because she combines sex with violence in a way they aren't accustomed to and don't much like.

Then there are figures like Hawthorne's adulterous Hester Prynne, she of the scarlet letter, who becomes a kind of sex saint through suffering. We assume she did what she did for love, and thus she becomes a good woman who did a bad thing for a good reason. And Madame Bovary, who not only indulged her romantic temperament and voluptuous, sensual appetites but also spent too much of her husband's money doing it, which was her downfall. A good course in double-entry bookkeeping would have saved the day. I suppose she is a foolish woman who did a stupid thing for an insufficient reason, since the men in question were dolts. Neither the modern reader nor the author considers her evil, though many contemporaries did, as you can see if you read the transcript of the court case in which the forces of moral rectitude tried to get the book censored.

One of my favorite bad women is Becky Sharp of Thackeray's *Vanity Fair*. She makes no pretensions to goodness. She is wicked; she enjoys being wicked; and she does it out of vanity and for her own profit, tricking and deluding English society in the process, which, the author implies, deserves to be tricked and deluded, since it is hypocritical and selfish to the core. Thackeray obviously prefers Becky to the goody-goody Amelia, and doesn't even punish her much at the end. She's a bad mother, too, and that's a whole other subject: bad mothers and wicked stepmothers and oppressive aunts like the one in *Jane Eyre*, and nasty female teachers and depraved governesses and evil grannies. The possibilities are many.

But I think that's enough reprehensible behavior for you. Life is short, art is long, motives are complex, and human nature is endlessly fascinating and inventive. Many doors stand ajar. What is in the forbidden room? Something different for everyone, but something you need to know and will never find out unless you step across the threshold. If you are a man, the bad female character in a novel may be, in Jungian terms, your anima, but if you're a woman, the bad female character is your shadow, and as we know from reading Hoffmann, she who loses her shadow also loses her soul.

I will leave you with two quotations. One is from the aptly named Lewis Hyde: "The trickster becomes the messenger of the gods." The second is from Dame Rebecca West, speaking in 1912: "Ladies of Great Britain, we have not enough evil in us." Note where the evil is located: in us.

No, But I Saw the Movie

RUSSELL BANKS

December 9, 1999

For many years, or maybe not so many—for some years, anyhow—
I'd be out on the book-tour hustings and after reading would be
signing books at a table in the lobby, and a lovely thing would happen. A stranger, a total stranger, would appear in line and volunteer
that he or she loved one of my books (one other than the book that
I was at that moment signing, of course, and was now embellishing
with endearments and fawning declarations of lifelong gratitude).
There is, of course, nothing more satisfying to an author of serious
literary fiction or poetry—which is to say, an author who does not
write for money—than to be told by a stranger that one's work has
entered that stranger's life.

And whenever a person told me that he or she had enjoyed
Affliction, say, or *The Sweet Hereafter*, I assumed the reference was
to my book, and I might say in a surprised way—for it was, after
all, to me still somewhat surprising—"Oh? You read the book?" As

if the reference were possibly to another affliction, like cholera or extreme poverty, or to a different Sweet Hereafter, a designer drug, maybe, or a chic new soul-food restaurant on Manhattan's Upper West Side. Inviting, I suppose, what usually followed, which was a description of the circumstances or conditions under which the book was read—a book club, my brother-in-law gave it to me for Christmas, a college course, I read it in prison, in the hospital, on a train/plane/slow boat to China, etcetera.

It's what we talk about when we talk about a book that one of us has written and the other has read. We're inevitably somewhat self-conscious, at a loss for the appropriate words, in a bit of a blush, both of us. Writing and reading literary fiction and poetry are activities almost too intimate to talk about. Literature is intimate behavior between strangers, possibly more intimate even than sex, and it occurs between *extreme* strangers, who sometimes do not even speak the same language and thus require the services of a translator. Sometimes one of the strangers (the writer, usually) has been dead for centuries; sometimes he or she is utterly unknown, anonymous, or someone, like Homer or the author of the Upanishads or the Song of Solomon, whose individual identity has been mythologized and absorbed by an entire people.

My point is simply that this activity of writing involves at its center the desire on the part of the writer to become intimate with strangers, to speak from one's secret, most vulnerable, truth-telling self directly to a stranger's same self. And it's so central to the impulse that it actually does not work when one's readers are *not* strangers, when one's readers are one's friends, lovers, or family members (it's well known, after all, that no writer takes pleasure from the praise of his mom or kid sister, and we're all conditioned from our apprenticeship on not to take seriously the critiques offered by our husbands and wives and best friends). Either way, people who know us personally have motives and knowledge that disqualify them as readers. No, it's only the kindness of strangers that counts, that shyly offered gift, "I have read your novel." (With the clear implication, of course, that it was not an unhappy or unrewarding experience.)

I know this because I am a reader, too. I am other writers' intimate stranger, and I have sat next to an author at dinner and have felt the same odd, embarrassing need to declare, as if revealing a slightly illicit or inappropriate interest in baseball cards or negligee mail-order catalogs, that I have read his or her novel, and I know that, in saying so, I am confessing that I have traveled out of body deeply into that stranger's fictional world and have resided there, dreamed there, hallucinated there, and have been moved, comforted, and frightened, have laughed aloud there and maybe even wept. The author, I can always tell, is slightly embarrassed by my confession, but pleased nonetheless—the more so inasmuch as he or she and I have never met before and never will again, and he or she has never read anything of mine and, if the author wishes to preserve our beautiful relationship as it is, never will, either. Reader and writer from two different solar systems, our orbits intersect for a second, and we reflect back the flash of each other's light, take brief comfort from the actual physical existence of the other, and then speed on, safely back in our own imagined universe, as if the other were not circling far away in another universe, around a different, possibly brighter sun than ours.

In the last few years, however, there has been a subtle but important change for me in this exchange between writer and presumed reader. Nowadays, when at the book-signing table, I'm often approached by a person carrying a copy of *Affliction*, for example, the paperback with the picture of Nick Nolte and James Coburn on the cover, or maybe the Canadian edition of *The Sweet*

Hereafter with Ian Holm and Sarah Polley staring mournfully out, and the person will say, "I loved *Affliction*," or, "*The Sweet Hereafter* meant a lot to me," and pleased and slightly embarrassed, as usual, I will say, "Oh? You read the book?" And the person will look at me somewhat quizzically, and say, "Uh . . . no, but I saw the movie."

I honestly don't know how that makes me feel, how I *ought* to feel, or what I ought to say in response. What *do* we talk about when we talk about a book I wrote whose movie version you saw? Or a book I wrote that you know of solely because you heard about the movie and saw the clips on the Academy Awards? What is the relationship generally between literary fiction (that relatively esoteric art form) and film (the most popular and powerful art form of our time), and in particular between my literary fictions and their film adaptations?

These are not simple questions, and literary writers have historically been reluctant to discuss them, except in dismissive ways. Hemingway famously advised novelists to drive (*presumably* from the east) to the California-Nevada state line and toss the novel over the line, let the movie people toss the money back, then turn around and drive away as fast as possible. Which is what most novelists have done, and is what most producers, directors, screenwriters, and actors have wanted them to do. Let us buy your plot, they say, your characters, setting, themes, and language, and do whatever we please with them; that's what the money's *for*, Mr. Shakespeare, so we can leave dear old Lear happily ensconced at the Linger Longer Assisted-Living Facility in Naples, Florida, with his three daughters, Melanie, Gwyneth, and Julia, living together in adjoining condos nearby, heavily into Gulf Coast real estate, romance on the horizon, fade out and hit the credits soundtrack, "Stayin' Alive" by the Bee Gees, and let's get Newman for the old guy, and for his pal, whatzisname, the guy with glaucoma, get Jack—we'll keep the title, sort of, only we'll call it *Shake-speare in Retirement*.

Writers who didn't, or couldn't, afford to take Hemingway's advice almost always paid for it dearly with their pride, their integrity, often their reputations, and sometimes even their whole careers. The story is that Hollywood is like Las Vegas—if you have a weakness, they'll find it. Everyone knows Fitzgerald's sad tale of depression, booze, and crack-up, and there are dozens more. Faulkner seems to have managed only by staying solidly drunk from arrival to departure. Nelson Algren sold the film rights of *The Man with the Golden Arm* to Otto Preminger, contingent on Algren's being hired to write the screenplay; later, safely back in Chicago, he said, "I went out there for a thousand a week, and I worked Monday, and I got fired Wednesday. The guy that hired me was out of town on Tuesday." S. J. Perelman said of Hollywood, "It was a hideous and untenable place when I dwelt there, popu-lated with few exceptions by Yahoos, and now that it has become the chief citadel of television, it's unspeakable." A native of Provi-dence, Rhode Island, and a great writer about boxing and horse racing, you'd not think of Perelman as especially fastidious, but Hollywood he saw as "a dreary industrial town controlled by hood-lums of enormous wealth, the ethical sense of a pack of jackals, and taste so degraded that it befouled everything it touched." (Sort of the way I see Providence, now that I think of it.) More or less in the same vein, John Cheever said, "My principal feeling about Hollywood is suicide. If I could get out of bed and into the shower, I was all right. Since I never paid the bills, I'd reach for the phone and order the most elaborate breakfast I could think of, and then I'd try to make it to the shower before I hanged myself." Strong statements, but not at all atypical, when serious literary writers found themselves obliged to work in, for, and with the makers of movies. Ben Hecht put it in depressingly simple terms: "I'm a Hollywood writer; so I put on a sports jacket and take off my brain."

And yet, one is forced to ask, was that then and this is now? And how do we account for the difference? Because, when one looks around today, one notices an awful lot of very respectable fiction writers having what appears to be a very good time in bed with Hollywood, both as authors of novels adapted to film, like Michael Ondaatje's *The English Patient*, Toni Morrison's *Beloved*, Peter Carey's *Oscar and Lucinda*, David Guterson's *Snow Falling on Cedars*, and Mona Simpson's *Anywhere but Here*, and as fiction writers turned screenwriters, like Richard Price, John Irving, Amy Tan, Jim Harrison, and Susan Minot. Paul Auster has even *directed* his first film and is planning to try a second. There are others waiting in the wings. And we're not talking about the Crichtons and the Clancys here, whose fiction seems written mainly to fit the template of blockbuster movies—a respectable line of work, but not one I myself identify with. No, we're talking about writers whose fiction aspires to the somewhat more Parnassian heights where literature resides, work composed without consideration of financial reward and meant to be compared, for better or worse, to the great literary works of the past. And there is a growing phalanx of such writers, whose often difficult, morally ambiguous novels—complexly layered books with unruly characters—have been eagerly sought out and adapted for film. I honestly can't remember a period like it. We could easily make a very long list of novelists and story writers—serious, literary writers—almost none of whom actually live and work in Hollywood, as it happens (thanks to fax machine, modem, and e-mail), but all of whom are making a fairly good living from the film industry these days, a much better living, certainly, than they could make on the sales of their books alone or than many of them used to make teaching in university creative-writing programs.

I now must add my own name to that list, and confess that in the last few years, not only have I made a pretty good living from the movie business, I've had a heck of a good time doing it, too. And furthermore, I'm not ashamed or even slightly embarrassed by the movies that have been adapted from my novels. Well, that's not altogether true: there are a few moments in each that make me cringe and crouch low in my seat when I see them. But overall I am delighted to have been associated with the making of those two films, *Affliction* and *The Sweet Hereafter*, and I am grateful to the people who made them and to the businesspeople who financed them. I think they are interesting, excellent films on their own terms, and I feel they honor the novels on which they are based. And I don't believe I'm alone in having had such a delightful experience—most of the writers I listed earlier, if not all of them, feel the same about the films adapted from their works. Oh, Rick Moody might grumble about aspects of *The Ice Storm* and William Kennedy might quibble with some of the decisions made in the making of *Ironweed*, but unlike the Faulkners, Cheevers, Perelmans, and Hechts of previous generations, none of the writers mentioned here feels demeaned, exploited, or deceived. The contrast between my experience and that of so many of my colleagues, on the one hand, and the experience of our predecessors, on the other, is so great as to raise an interesting question. Simply, has the movie industry in the last ten or fifteen years, and especially in the last five years, become uncharacteristically hospitable to serious works of fiction, or have the sensibilities and needs of the writers of fiction been coarsened and dumbed down to such a degree that they no longer feel offended by Hollywood?

Obviously—since, rightly or wrongly, I feel neither coarsened nor especially dumbed down—I believe it's the former. It's Hollywood that's changed. And it's possible that my own experience there, since it hasn't been especially uncharacteristic, can illustrate how it has changed, if not suggest why. Although *Affliction* was not released until December 1998, and *The Sweet Hereafter* was released a year earlier, in December 1997, both movies were shot within weeks of each other between January and March of 1997. Both were filmed in Canada, *Affliction* in Quebec, less than two hours' drive from my home in upstate New York, and *The Sweet Hereafter* in Toronto and British Columbia. The most salient aspect of this (other than the fact that, because they were nearby, I got to hang around the sets a whole lot) is merely that neither movie was filmed in Los Angeles. A far more important fact, however, is that the director of *Affliction*, Paul Schrader, and the director of *The Sweet Hereafter*, Atom Egoyan, although a generation apart, are both auteur-style independent filmmakers, serious cinematic artists with highly developed artistic imaginations. Crucially, they are men with no studio affiliations who finance their projects by hook and crook, pasting together support from half a dozen sources, foreign and domestic, risking their mortgages, their kids' college educations, and next summer's vacation every time out, in a game that for them is high stakes and personal but leaves them with maximum control over what ends up on the screen. Final cut, in other words, all the way down the line. And this is only possible because of budget size. Paul Schrader likes to point out that somewhere around fourteen million dollars you have to put white hats on the good guys and black hats on the bad guys. It's practically an immutable law of filmmaking. Fourteen million dollars, adjusted to inflation, is the point where you're told by the person with the checkbook: no more shades of gray, no more contradictions, no more ambiguities. *Affliction* cost a little over $6 million to make, *The Sweet Hereafter* cost about $4.7 million, and you can be sure that Nick Nolte, Sissy Spacek, James

Coburn, Willem Dafoe, and Ian Holm did not receive their usual fees. These actors—movie stars who command salaries equal, in a couple of cases, to the entire budget of the movie—worked for far less because they admired the director and the other cast members and wanted to work with them, they were excited by the screenplay and the source material for the film, and they wanted to portray characters who were colored in shades of gray, wanted to inhabit lives made complex and believable by contradiction and ambiguity, dealing with serious conflicts that matter in the real world. They believed in film as an art form and in their craft and the abilities of their colleagues, and were trying for that rare thing, a collaborative, lasting work of art.

Two important factors, then, contributed mightily to getting these rather difficult and, some might say, depressing films made: the directors, both of them artists with strong personal visions of the world, were independent filmmakers free of studio affiliation, with track records that attract great actors; and both films were budgeted low enough to keep down the debt service, so that an investor could recoup his money and even make a profit without having to sell tickets to every fourteen-year-old boy and girl in America. Without, in other words, having to turn the movie into a theme park or a video game. Also, there may have been a third factor that underlies both of these first two: technology. The technology of filmmaking has changed considerably in recent years. From the camera to the editing room, from the soundtrack to the projection booth, filmmaking has "gone digital," as they like to say, so that it's possible, for instance, as in *The Sweet Hereafter*, to send a school bus careening over a cliff and skidding across a frozen lake to where it stops, then slowly sinks below the ice, a horrifying sight—all composed in a few days in a dark room in Toronto, pixels on a computer screen, a *virtual* school bus, cliff, frozen lake, etcetera, for one-tenth the price and in one-quarter the time it would have taken to stage and film in 35 millimeter an *actual* bus, cliff, lake, etcetera. The enormous and incredibly expensive technological resources and hardware available to a studio will soon be available to almost any kid with a credit card or an indulgent uncle, and that kid can set up shop with a laptop anywhere—from Soho to Montreal to Toronto to Seattle—and compete with the Lucases, Disneys, and Hensons of the world.

American independent filmmaking seems to be entering a truly brave new world, and it will create a transition comparable, perhaps, to the transition between silent films and talkies, one in which, thanks to technological change, the old controlling economic structures undergo seismic shifts and rearrangements, with the result that the prevailing aesthetic and thematic conventions will have to give way. The boom in recent years of independent moviemaking is just the beginning. The trend toward multinational corporate bloat and gigantism will no doubt continue, if for no other reason than, thanks to the same technological change put to other uses, it *can*—unifying theme parks, professional sports, retailing, and gambling under one all-season stadium roof, so that the distinction between shopping and entertainment eventually disappears altogether, and Las Vegas and Orlando become our national cultural capitals, the twenty-first-century model cities of America. But at the same time, thanks to the very same technology, the equivalent of a cinematic samizdat is beginning to evolve right alongside it. This is where the real filmmaking is being done; the rest is little more than consumer advertising, tie-ins, and product placement. And this is where we'll see the bright young directors, screenwriters, cinematographers, and actors going to work. The Atom Egoyans and Paul Schraders of the future will be making their films rapidly and cheaply, editing them as fast as they're shot, and releasing them as independently as they're made, by the Internet or on video and DVD. Films like *The Blair Witch Project* and *Being John Malkovich* and *The Celebration* and the recently released *Last Night*—inventive, unconventionally structured, freshly and bravely imagined movies—are not anomalies in today's film world, although five years ago they would have been. Five years ago they probably would not have been made at all. Nor, for that matter, would *Affliction* and *The Sweet Hereafter*.

This is why, I think, you're seeing so many serious novelists hanging around the filmmakers these days. They sense there's something marvelous happening here and, if it doesn't take too much time away from their fiction writing and pays reasonably well, they'd like to be part of it. Just consider the writing itself. Until fairly recently, the conventions of screenwriting were, from a late twentieth-century novelist's perspective, moribund, stuck in linear time, glued to the old Aristotelian unities of place, time, and character, a three-act tale as anachronistic and predictable as . . . well, as a late nineteenth-century novel. What self-respecting postmodernist fiction writer would want to work in a form so limited and so inappropriate to our times? Yet for the writers of screenplays, until recently, it was as if, five generations after Faulkner, Joyce, and Woolf, modernism never existed, or if it did, it had no relevance to narrative except between the covers of a book. No wonder Ben Hecht felt he had to take his brain off when he went to work in Hollywood. No wonder Hemingway couldn't be bothered even to cross the state line. And no wonder there was such a fuss a few years ago when Quentin Tarantino, in *Pulp Fiction*, pushed the envelope a little and played with narrative time and point of view. At the time, it was a radical move for a screenwriter, perhaps, but all he was doing was employing a few of the tools that practically every second-year fiction-writing student keeps at the ready, switchback and replay, and a *Rashomon*-esque split point of view.

Consider again our two examples, *The Sweet Hereafter* and *Affliction*, not just how those screenplays were written, but the (to me) amazing fact that the novels were adapted for film at all. Never mind the subject matter—although it is amusing to imagine pitching the stories to an old-time studio executive. "Mr. Warner, I've got this very dark story that starts with a school bus accident in a small north-country town, and a large number of the children of the town are killed, and the movie is about the reaction of the village to this mind-numbing event." Or this: "An alcoholic, violent forty-five-year-old small-town cop tries and fails to overcome the psychological and moral disfigurement inflicted on him as a child by his alcoholic, violent father." The door, Mr. Banks, is over there.

Let's look at just the narrative form and structure of the two novels. *The Sweet Hereafter* is told from four separate, linked points of view, four different characters, each of whom picks up the story where the previous narrator left off and continues for seventy-five pages or so before handing it off, in the process remembering and recounting his or her past, offering reflections, ruminations, observations, and grief for the lost children. *Affliction* is told from the point of view of an apparently minor character who is gradually, indirectly, revealed to be an unreliable narrator and thus by the tale's end has become the central figure in the story, displacing the person we *thought* the story was about. Neither film lends itself to a conventional three-act screenplay with the usual plot points and fixed unities of time, place, and point of view, and if for no other reason than that (never mind subject matter), I was amazed that anyone even wanted to *try* to make a movie from them. Happily, both Egoyan and Schrader did, and they both felt free to invite me into the process of adaptation from the start and allowed me to look over their shoulders, as it were, all the way through to the editing room and beyond. It was fascinating and very instructive to see the liberties they took, not with the books, but with the old conventions of filmmaking, from screenplay to casting to camera placement to editing and sound.

For instance, to preserve the multiple points of view of *The Sweet Hereafter*—in the novel one can think of them as being structured vertically, like four columns of type, or four members of a mile relay team, which in the "real-time" constraints of a movie (as opposed to the more interactive "mental-time" freedoms of fiction) would have resulted in four separate, consecutive, thirty-minute movies—Egoyan essentially tipped the story onto its side, ran the several points of view horizontally, as it were, almost simultaneously, the relay runners running four abreast instead of sequentially, so that the story moves back and forth in time and from place to place with unapologetic ease.

Egoyan trusts his viewer to reconstruct time and place and reunify point of view on his or her own, just as one does when reading a modern novel. No big deal. Similarly, Schrader, with *Affliction*, felt no compunctions about letting the narrator of the novel, a minor character, it seems, one outside the action, function in the film as the witness and recapitulator of his older brother's deeds and misdeeds. This is the character who would surely have been eliminated at once from a studio production of this film, but Schrader makes him slowly, subtly, become the center of the story, using voice-over to establish his presence at every crucial juncture and giving us explicit, dramatized inconsistencies, conflicting versions of events, to establish his unreliability, so that Willem Dafoe's voice-over at the end, "Only I remain . . . ," can be heard and felt with a terrible chill of recognition by all of us in the audience, we who—unlike poor Wade Whitehouse, the ostensible and long-gone hero of our story—*also* remain. And in that way, the story of *Affliction* becomes our story; Wade's affliction becomes our culture's affliction.

Working closely with Egoyan and Schrader, I received a crash course in filmmaking, and what I learned *can't* be done in film was just as interesting and instructive to me, the fiction writer, as what I learned *can* be done in film was interesting and instructive to me, the neophyte screenwriter. A particularly useful, and typical, insight, for instance, came to me early on in the writing of *The Sweet Hereafter* screenplay. Egoyan had told me that one of the aspects of the novel that most excited him was the final scene, a demolition derby. We even drove to the Essex County Fair in upstate New York and videotaped one. It was the most cinematic scene in the book, Egoyan said. But when it came time to write it into the screenplay, he just couldn't. It was too big, too loud, too crowded, too crammed with action. What to do? He asked me, "What's the underlying function of the scene in the *novel?*" I explained that it served as a social rite, a familiar but strange, rigidly structured ritual that could embrace, embellish, and reconfigure the roles of the various members of the community. With the devices and artifices of fiction available to me, I could keep the noise down, thin out the crowd, slow down the speed—distancing the demolition derby so that it could function in the novel as an emblem for everything else in the story. He got this. Also, all along I'd told him that, to me, the novel only *seemed* realistic; that actually it was supposed to be experienced as a moral fable about the loss of the children in our culture, an elaboration on a medieval fairy tale. That's when he proposed cutting into the film the whole of the Browning poem "The Pied Piper of Hamelin," inserting a literal reading of the poem. At first I said no way, too literary. There's barely a mention of it in the book, one or two passing allusions, maybe. But the more I thought about it, the more I realized—too literary for a *novel*, maybe, but not for a film. Just as the demolition-derby scene was too cinematic for a film, maybe, but not for a novel. Film, I was discovering, is in your face; fiction is in your head.

Here's a further example: something I learned a full year after *The Sweet Hereafter* was released. In Toronto one night, Egoyan and I gave a presentation to benefit a small theater group there and decided that I would read scenes from the novel, and he would show clips of the film version of the same scenes, and then we'd discuss why we'd each done our respective work the way we did. One of these scenes was the incest scene, which a number of people who had, and some who hadn't, read the book complained about in the film. "It was like a dream," and "I thought maybe I'd imagined it," the fourteen-year-old Nichole tells us over and over in the novel—distancing us from the actual act, the incest, by placing her account of her *response* to it between it and us, so that we simultaneously imagine the act and the girl in two different time frames, both during and after. Egoyan tried to find a cinematic way to show that from Nichole's point of view it was like a dream, maybe something she'd imagined, etcetera, and as a result he presented it as if it *were* a dream, i.e., dreamy, with candles, music, a father who almost seems to be her boyfriend, which has the effect not of distancing the incest and allowing us to pity the victim and fear for her in an appropriate way, but of romanticizing it, making the victim seem way too complicit and fear and pity nearly impossible.

These lessons don't suggest to me that fiction is in any way superior to film. Merely different, in fascinating and challenging ways. Furthermore, the freedom to make movies this way, to be inventive, imaginative, and complex in the formal and structural aspects of the screenplay, and to deal with life-and-death issues that affect us all in our day-to-day lives, is what attracts novelists like Paul Auster, Peter Carey, John Irving, and so many others like them to the movie business. It's not, as in the past, merely the business of the movie business that attracts; it's the movies that can be made there. It's certainly what has attracted me. And as a direct result of my experience with *The Sweet Hereafter* and *Affliction*, I've become a screenwriter myself. And the people I'm working with, the directors, actors, producers, even the agents, are smart, and they are exceedingly skilled at what they do. They know all kinds of things that I don't, and in no way do they make me feel that, to work with them, I've got to put on a sports jacket and take off my brain. Quite the opposite.

Eudora Welty once said, "The novel is something that never was before and will not be again." That is the reason why we write them. When it begins to appear that a film can also be that new, that uniquely itself, then, believe me, men and women who otherwise would be writing novels will want to make films, too. We are fast approaching that point. Oh, sure, it is a lot of fun to hobnob with movie stars and go to Cannes and Sundance and ride to the Oscars in a limo the likes of which you haven't seen since your senior prom, but the thrill fades faster than cheap cologne. The thrill of becoming intricately and intimately involved in the process of making a true work of narrative art, however, and the chance to make that work of art collaboratively in the most powerful medium known to mankind, that's as thrilling as it gets, at least for this old storyteller it is. And, too, as Peter De Vries once said, "I love being a writer. What I can't stand is the paperwork."

But I don't want to leave the mistaken impression that I or any of the other novelists I've mentioned, my blessed colleagues, is likely to give up writing fiction to devote him- or herself to film.

Despite the paperwork. That's inconceivable to me. These dalliances with film—however thrilling, remunerative, and instructive they are—can't replace the deep, life-shaping, life-*changing* response one gets from creating a fictional world, living in that world for years at a time, then sending it out to strangers. *Perfect* strangers. A novel, like a marriage, can change your life for the rest of your life; I'm not so sure that can be said of a movie, any more than it can of a love affair.

What, then, *do* I say to that very kind stranger who tells me, "No, but I saw the movie"? I can answer, "Ah, but that was in another country, friend, and in a different time. If you read the book, you will now and then be reminded of that country, perhaps, and that time, but only dimly and incidentally." For when we open a novel, we bring to it everything that we bring to a film: our memories and fears and our longings and dreams, our secrets (even the ones we keep from ourselves)—all of which the film either displaces or simply disregards as it unspools in the dark before us. All of which—our memories, fears, longings, and dreams—the novel engages and utilizes wholly as it takes us out of our lives into another that's as much of our own making as it is of the novelist's. That intimacy, that secret sharing among strangers, is what no novelist and no reader can give up. No matter how remarkable it is, a film is what it is, regardless of our presence or absence before it. The darkened theater can be empty, and it won't affect the essential nature of the film being shown there. But a novel simply does not exist until it's read, and each time it's read, even if it's read a second time by the same person, or a third, even if it's read a thousand years after it was written, it's just as Eudora Welty said, it is "something that never was before and will not be again."

Childhood of a Writer

E. L. DOCTOROW

March 13, 1991

I was given the name Edgar because my father loved the work of Edgar Allan Poe. Actually he liked James Fenimore Cooper too—in fact he liked a lot of bad writers—but I am consoled because Poe is our greatest bad writer. Just a few years ago I said to my aged mother, "Did you and Dad realize you were naming me after an alcoholic, drug-addicted, delusional paranoid with strong necrophiliac tendencies?" "Edgar," she replied, "that's not funny."

Of course as a child I was aware of none of this, nor of the fact that Poe, with the American nation in full bloom all around him, detested its democratic masses, preferring the aristocratic torment of his own solipsistic mind, which he projected as the dungeons, caskets, airless rooms, and other stultifying containers of his tales. In time I too would come to love this brilliant hack, this impoverished visionary, this contentious critic embattled in the literary life of his day. An immigrant New Yorker, with a palpable distaste for New England literary Brahmins, he went his own resentful way as a poet of lost loves and psychologist of the perverse. But in my childhood all I knew was that my parents had named me after a writer so famous that he was included in the deck of *Authors*, a popular card guessing game.

Naming is profoundly important, every name carrying an injunction and so, if coordinate enough with other circumstances of life, a fate. Not in my case, fortunately, to take drugs or to drink myself blind. But along with my literary name I found myself in a household of books, shelves of them, my parents' books, my older brother's books, the books my mother brought home from the rental library in the corner drugstore. And then there were the books I myself brought in by the armful every week from the New York Public Library branch on Washington Avenue in the Bronx.

When at the age of eight I was hospitalized with a burst appendix, I was given a new kind of book just then coming out, a book that could fit into your pocket, a pocket book or paperback that cost only twenty-five cents. Not knowing myself to be on the verge of death, I read in the interstices of my deliriums *Bring 'Em Back Alive* by Frank Buck, a scurrilous self-promoting white supremacist zoo supplier; *Bambi* by a bloodless Austrian writer named Felix Salten, as only someone bloodless could have written that insipid tale of a deer; then a not entirely reputable novel of Eastern mysticism by James Hilton, *Lost Horizon*, my introduction to the idea of a non-materialistic and therefore quite boring heaven on earth; and finally *Wuthering Heights*, a novel about adult matters that did not interest me. These were among the first ten titles released by Pocket Books, a new idea in American publishing stolen from the Europeans, and I still have them and remember their being placed on my bedside table by my pale wan worried mother and father as amulets to see me through it, whose love for their wretched sick child comes back to me at this advanced age—that light we live in and see by, if we're lucky, but only come to see, not when in our shared adulthood with our parents neither we nor they particularly remember it, but after their death, when that is what keeps living, that steady and irreducible light.

How understandable is it that in my early twenties, out of the army, married with a child of my own, I hungrily sought and found employment as an editor with another publisher of mass paperback books, New American Library—the Signet line, the Mentor line—in what turned out to be the heyday of the mass market paperback, by then seventy-five cents or as much as a dollar and a quarter for the thick ones. I was cool enough not to reveal my larcenous excitement in having all these books to hand, and in getting paid to find and read good books and buy the rights and print up a hundred thousand, say, of a good obscure first novel, give it a jazzy cover, and ship it out to all the airports in the country, all the drugstores and railroad stations, for people to buy for pocket change in those days when you could find a consequential mass market book, not a genre romance, not an assembly-line technothriller, but a book—Pasternak's *Doctor Zhivago*, Ralph Ellison's *Invisible Man*—"Good Reading for the Masses" as the publisher promised, of the kind my parents intended me to have when I was in the hospital in danger of dying.

I was sent off to the suburb of Pelham Manor to convalesce in a quiet stately home, the domain of a quiet stately aunt, she, and her home, teaching me the necessary and sufficient conditions of a life of calmness, of soft-spoken speech. These were: space, live-in servants, clean windows with the sunlight shining through, and trees and grass and a flower garden outside the windows, none of which were available to my parents in their Bronx flat, home also to my mother's unemployed brother, a musician, the once successful leader of a swing orchestra, and my ancient grandmother, who was given to spells of madness. My parents, though united in their love for me and for my older brother, were otherwise in perpetual and highly vocal disagreement about how to survive in the Depression, the qualities of character it demanded . . . and whatever the benefits of my home life, peacefulness and the calm address were not among them. In my loyalty to my family, and possibly a subliminal fascination with the clutch of disparate personalities I lived among, all of them exemplars of the vivid communication, demonstrators of the powers to be achieved from abutting the Latin and the Anglo-Saxon, and with rare and so all the more effective recourse to the Yiddish, I felt estranged and possibly neglected in such suburban comfort and peace and quiet as my gentle aunt provided, and so took to the bookshelves of my cousin, away at college with her children's library left behind, and ploughed through the collected Oz novels of L. Frank Baum. A few years ago I read that Baum was a communist, and that the Oz stories can be read as an allegory of Communist idealism, the godlike Wizard being an admitted fraud, a temporary expedient, a ruling vanguard, you see, with the power really residing in the people if they would only come to realize it, though it takes a bit of traveling to get there . . . an interpretation I would have found quite useless had I known of it, especially as I was reading the book in the comfortable home of my aunt and uncle, he, I should say, a rock-ribbed Republican of such probity as hardly to countenance in his home a work of inflammatory literature directed at his own daughter. Additionally, I am skeptical. I don't question the fact of Baum's politics or even his intentions, though we know by now that an author's intentions are hardly reliable measures of his accomplishments; but the images of which the Oz books are constructed are so vivid and original as virtually to wipe out any referential meanings that would arise. Besides which, my cousin, in whose room I slept, was a fancier of dogs, she had raised a champion Kerry blue terrier, its blue ribbons went around the four walls of the room like a cove molding, and on her shelves along with Baum were several of the canine novels of Albert Payson Terhune, whose hero dogs always managed to save their owners' wealthy mansions from the depredations of evil interlopers, usually African American. These tales, so in sync with the prevailing social attitudes in the town of Pelham Manor, county of Westchester, 1939, were not visibly racist to the unraised consciousnesses of white God-fearing circumspection in my aunt's peaceful house. Terhune's volumes far outnumbered those of L. Frank Baum, and what I took from them was something else entirely, the literary possibilities in attributing human emotions to an animal.

Back home, and more or less on my feet again, I took out of the public library the two great dog novels of Jack London, published together for my convenience in one sturdy library binding, *The Call of the Wild* and *White Fang*, the one about a civilized dog who is kidnapped and enslaved as a sled-husky in the Yukon and, under the brutal pressures of human masters, finds freedom and self-realization in reverting to the primeval wolf ways of his remote ancestry, the other about a savage wolf who, under the ministrations of a decent human being, becomes a civilized human-friendly dog. He was nothing, Jack London, if not a writer who knew a good formula when he found one. On tales such as these he became the most popular writer in America, and he is still widely read around the world, though he sits at literature's table below the salt while the more sophisticated voices of modernist and postmodernist irony conduct the conversation.

The tests and trials to which Buck, the dog in *The Call of the Wild*, is subjected, and the way he meets them and learns and grows in moral stature, make Buck a round character, while the human beings in the book are, in their constant one-note villainy, flat. That is irony too, a fine irony. Furthermore, this little speed-readers' novel, written at the level of a good pulp serial, is in fact a parody of the novel of sentimental education, not only because the hero is a dog, but because his education decivilizes him, turns him back into the wild creature of his primordial ancestry. I appreciate that now, but then I only knew Jack London was different from the picture-book writer Aesop, he was not tiresome as Aesop was, he took animals seriously, granting them complex character as the veterinarily incorrect Aesop never did. The moral of the Jack London book was not something you knew already without having to be instructed. But it was there and it was resonant with my own life. Every day, it seemed, old men knocked on the front door to ask my mother for money to help bring Jews out of Europe. Playing with my friends in the park, I had to watch out for older boys who swept up from the East Bronx to take at knifepoint our spaldines and whatever pocket change we were carrying. My father, the proud owner of a music shop in the old Hippodrome theater at Sixth Avenue and Forty-Third Street, a man who knew the classical repertoire inside out and stocked music that nobody else had, a man whom the great artists of the day consulted for their record purchases, lost his store in the "little" Depression of 1940. My ancient grandmother, growing more and more insane each day, now ran away to wander the streets until the police found her and brought her home. We were broke, what the newspapers called war clouds were growing darker and more ominous, my brother was of freshly minted draft age, and *The Call of the Wild*, this mordant parable of the thinness of civilization, the savagery bursting through as the season changed in the Bronx and a winter of deep heavy snows, like the snows of the Yukon, fell upon us, the whole city muffled and still, made me long to be in the wild, loping at the head of my pack, ready to leap up and plunge my incisors into the throats of all who would harm me or my family.

At one point I must have realized the primordial power belonged not only to the dog, or not in fact to the dog, because around this time—I was perhaps nine years old—I decided I was a writer. It was a clear conviction, not even requiring a sacred vow; I assumed the identity with grace, as one slips on a jacket or sweater that fits perfectly. It was such a natural assumption of my mind that for several years I felt no obligation actually to write anything. My convalescence had left me flabby, out of shape, with less energy for running around. I was more disposed than ever to read or listen to radio stories, and I was now reading not only to find out what happened next but with that additional line of inquiry of the child writer who is yet to write: *How is this done?* It is a kind of imprinting. We live in the book as we read it, yes, but we run with the author as well—this wild begetter of voices, this voice of voices, this noble creature of the wild whose linguistic lope over any sort of terrain brings it into being.

Understandably, in a season of gloom and menace, I soon achieved a taste for horror stories—Poe, naturally, W. W. Jacobs, Mary Shelley, Saki, and even the bloodier vendors of the comic book tales. My father was not too distracted with worry to notice this, and he was not without a sense of humor. He handed me a book from the bookcase in my grandparents' apartment when we were visiting one Sunday afternoon: "Here, since you like all that horror stuff, here's one called *The Green Hand*. Sounds good and horrible to me." While all the grown-ups were having tea I sat in a corner and opened this book, and of course it wasn't a horror story about some disembodied, gangrenous green hand, it was a novel about a novice aboard a sailing ship, a *greenhand*. So by means of my father's trickery I fell to reading nothing but sea stories. That particular volume was one of a set of sea novels my grandfather had—*The Wreck of the Grosvenor, Captain Marryat, Moby-Dick,* and so on. I was to go through them all.

My grandfather had a personal library of books he'd picked up over the years in various kinds of promotions: book sets and encyclopedias, multivolume histories like the *Harper's History of the Civil War,* masterworks of all ages in uniform editions with titles like *The World's Great Orations.* My grandfather was a printer who had come here from Russia as a young man in 1885. In those days books were premiums you collected coupons for when you bought other things, including the daily newspaper. And all the immigrants who were trying to catch up as fast as possible collected these books. But he'd always been a great reader, my grandfather, and among his few precious possessions that he brought over with him in steerage were his books in Russian and in Yiddish. It was from my grandfather that I first heard the name Tolstoy—Lev Tolstoy he called him. One day he recounted to me Tolstoy's not exactly appropriate story for a child's ear, *The Death of Ivan Ilyich,* which describes in detail what it feels like to die. But he was right, I was fascinated. Another time he made me a present of one of his books, Tom Paine's *The Age of Reason,* a scornful dismissal of biblical fundamentalism. "My own mind is my church," Paine says, announcing his blasphemous Deism. It was this book among other rowdy acts that made the great writing hero of the American Revolution an embarrassment to the new government. My grandfather presented me with his copy around the time I was studying for my bar mitzvah. For among other tensions in my wonderful family was an irresolvable religious conflict, the generations of men, my grandfather, my father, being skeptics, the women, my grandmothers, my mother, being to one degree or another observant, keepers of dietary laws, lovers of the Sabbath, candle lighters, fasters on the High Holy Days, and so on.

Nowadays educators, psychologists speak of the ideal of the enriched childhood, and I see how enriched mine was amid these hard-living adults who struggled to pay the rent and put food on the table. But how could I or any of us know how enriching it all was—it was life, that's all, it was normal, feverishly expressive burgeoning life. Our underfinanced household was filled with music, not only my father's extensive record collection, to which, if I was careful handling the breakable 78s in their sleeves, I had unrestricted access, but my mother's pianistics, for she was a consummate musician, the daughter of musicians, whose disquieted soul found solace in the most tempestuous pieces of Chopin—the Revolutionary Etude, for example, that thunderously rolling earthquake of a composition. My older brother played jazz piano and organized a band that rehearsed in the front parlor also known as the sunroom. Music of all kinds and periods filled my home and my head. And though I never took to it as a discipline, having dismayed everyone within hearing when I sat down to practice my piano lessons, somehow the difference between notes on a staff and words on a page must have elided in my child's mind, which may be why in my working life those aroused mental states from which books begin are as likely to be evoked by a phrase in music as by the music I hear in words.

It is true also that everyone in my family seemed to be a good storyteller, every one of them without exception. They were persons to whom interesting things seemed to happen. The events they spoke of were most often of a daily, ordinary sort, but when composed and narrated, of great importance and meaning. Of course when you bring love to the person you're listening to, a story has to be interesting, and in one sense the challenge to a professional writer of books is to overcome the disadvantage of not being someone the reader knows and loves. But apart from that, the family of storytellers I listened to must have had a very firm view of themselves in the world. Otherwise they could not have done it so well. They were authorities of their own lives. They were strong enough presences in their own minds to trust that people would attend to them when they spoke. In fact their narratives were often accounts of their struggle for recognition of the worth they felt in themselves . . . or briefs against the lack of recognition they were receiving from others. There was no end to the varieties of myths they could construct from the realities of their relationships with one another.

Without realizing it I was spending a good part of my childhood listening quite carefully to the conversations of adults, even on those occasions when I was not known to be listening. And I particularly attended to the use of words at moments of high emotion, even when that emotion, anger, for instance, was directed at me. I appreciated idiomatic usages, and I understood the different pacts between speaker and listener, the different dictions, according to the formality or intimacy of the situation.

I may have been making some connection between the stories I heard spoken—the voiced stories—and the books I was reading whose voices played out in my mind. But I doubt that I would have understood that the writers of published books made themselves from what has to be a universal capacity for storytelling. That whereas an aptitude for mathematics or physics is given to relatively few, narrative seems to be within everyone's grasp, perhaps because it was the very first means people ever had to understand who they were and what was happening to them.

I have held to an idea ever since I heard it posited by one of my professors at Kenyon College in the fifties: that there was an ancient time when no distinction was possible between fact and fiction, between religious perception and scientific discourse, between utilitarian communication and poetry—when all these functions of language, which we now divide and distinguish according to the situation we're in, were indivisible. As in Homer. As in Genesis. This was reported to me as the Holophrastic theory of language and the image provided was of a star, the points being where we are today, the center being of that early linguistically imploded time. I don't know who came up with this idea or if it is still bandied about in seminars or if it has gone out of fashion or been modified to compatibility by cultural studies constructionists. But verifiable or not, it satisfies me because it explains why even as we live in an age that is scientifically oriented, even as we hold to the values of empiricism, demanding of our propositions that they be tested and of our legal cases that they rest on demonstrable evidence, our modern minds are still structured for storytelling. Facts may change, evolve, they do so all the time, but stories find their way to the unchanging core of things. People think naturally in terms of conflict and its resolution and in terms of character undergoing events, and of the outcomes of events being not at all sure, and therefore suspenseful . . . and the whole thing done moreover from a confidence of narrative that must belong to us and to our brains as surely as we are predisposed to the protocols of grammar.

If you want to test this particular proposition you cannot do better than to read some works of oral history. I remember reading from one collection—I don't have the title to hand—of pieces by women who settled on the Kansas frontier in the nineteenth century where they and their families were subjected to floods, droughts, plagues of locusts, and a series of topical ailments, most prominently ague, which we would call malaria. There's a line I've never forgotten from one of these women speaking of a neighboring family: "When Mr. Briggs was so with it [the ague] that Mrs. Briggs had to cut the wood, she put the baby behind him on the corded bedstead where his shivering joggled the baby off to sleep."

This writer knew, this neighbor of the Briggses, what that master theorist of fiction, Flaubert, had articulated as a kind of discovery: that the way to make an object in fiction exist is to have it worked upon by another object. What makes things come into being is their transaction. Mr. Briggs's illness exists because he shivers, the bed exists because he lies upon it, and the sleeping baby exists because his father's malarial convulsions rock the bedstead. But this writer knew more—and so we learn from Mrs. Briggs's action a good deal of her character, her enterprise in using even her husband's illness in their daily struggle for survival on the prairie. We know this life is harsh. We can imagine from this sentence alone the homemade nature of the house, perhaps even what things look like outside the house, and in fact we may derive from it the entire character of life on the American frontier in the mid-nineteenth century.

For all of that, though, books are books, meaning that unlike people they can detail the whole three hundred and sixty degrees from birth to death. And who in the world can tell a story as well as Mark Twain and Charles Dickens? I found *David Copperfield* in my parents' library—two volumes in the flexible black binding of the Harvard Classics, the five-foot shelf assembled by Charles W. Eliot just for me. Others of Dickens's works I pulled from the shelves of the public library branch on Washington Avenue. It was a bit of a walk from my house to the library, and fittingly enough, to get there I had to pass a bread-baking factory from which issued the delicious smells of fresh baking rye and pumpernickel. The copy of *Great Expectations* in its stiff library binding had been taken out so many times the pages had a soft pliant feel to them, like cloth.

Dickens did not disdain to write about children. Oliver, Pip, David Copperfield himself were abused and denied their rightful patrimony, or fell into an inheritance by some act of grace of their own, but there were others not so lucky. Yet Dickens was not what you would call a children's author. The terms of his children's fates were entirely adult terms—they would succeed to estate, education, the upper class, or they would not. Twain, with *The Adventures of Tom Sawyer*, was more likely to be regarded as a children's author—he chafed under the identification and had to be persuaded not to publish this work as a book for adults—because his children, in contrast to those of Dickens, usually made their own terms for their lives. They were never destined for adulthood. On the contrary, they lived in their own universe, out in the open under the sun. They were democrats and were celebrated as such. Only the detestable Sid, Tom Sawyer's hypocritical devious lying half brother, a descendant in fact of Tom Jones's pusillanimous half brother Blifil in Fielding's great work—only Sid could have made a home for himself in London, the other never. Twain does set *The Prince and the Pauper* in sixteenth-century England, but that story turns out to be the most precise symbolic presentation of the democratic ideal imaginable because the two boys, Tom Canty and the Prince, are seen to be interchangeable, each one, pauper and prince, functioning quite well as the other, and what is being said is anti-European and antimonarchical—that a society of class distinctions is essentially a fraud.

But with what a thrill of recognition I read my own feelings as they were rendered in *Tom Sawyer*: Tom's aversion to soap and water; his keen interest in the insect forms of life; his not always kind attention to dogs and cats; how he found solace from the unjust judgment of an Aunt Polly by dreaming of running away; how he loved Becky Thatcher, the sort of simpering little blonde I too fell for in grade school; how he did the absolutely right thing in taking her punishment at school to protect her. But most of all, without consciously realizing it, I had to have recognized the truth of the taxonomic world Tom Sawyer lived in, because it was so in accord with my own, a world of two distinct and for the most part irreconcilable life forms, the Child and the Adult, which are nevertheless united in times of crisis. And it is no small thing for a child who understands, at whatever degree of consciousness, that his own transgressions—and mine were seemingly endless, from dangerous illnesses to bad grades to unprepared piano lessons—are never as dire as they seem, and that there is a bond that unites old and young in one moral world in which truth can be realized and forgiveness is always possible.

If you look at *Tom Sawyer* today, in your adulthood, it is of course a completely different book. Tom is a mysterious fellow, an anthropological construct, and more a pastiche of boyhood qualities than a boy. He is pliant, behaving as a five-year-old or a fifteen-year-old as his adventures demand. He's a morally plastic trickster in part derived from the Trickster myths of the African American and Native American traditions. He's a god of mischief, who arranges the course of history to bring honor to himself . . . and if I now feel less favorably disposed toward him than I once did it is probably because of his own reprehensible behavior in *Huckleberry Finn*, a novel whose ending he completely ruins.

Among Virginia Woolf's collected essays is a talk she gave at a school entitled "How Should One Read a Book?" "Try to become [the author]," she advises:

> Be his fellow worker and accomplice . . . the chapters of a novel
> are an attempt to make something as formed and controlled as a
> building: but words are more impalpable than bricks . . . Perhaps

the quickest way to understand the elements of what a novelist is doing is not to read, but to write; to make your own experiment with the dangers and difficulties of words.

And so I did, finally, get around to writing, after the war had begun, and my brother was off somewhere overseas, and my father, working now as a salesman, read the news each evening, buying up every paper he could get his hands on. I was in junior high school, sometimes called middle school, seventh to ninth grade. Little pennants with blue stars had appeared in all the windows of the neighborhood, and sometimes gold stars as well, and the newsreels in the movie houses showed the tanks rumbling, the bombs falling, the ships' guns firing, while I, having been named after Poe, took to writing in the hermetic tradition, setting my stories in dungeons or dark houses that lacked central heating. They began with lines like "The cell was dark and dank."

After my Poe period I lay fallow for a while. Ideas came to me as sudden arousals of the brain, cerebral excitements that I would attempt to convert to a plot or situation, trying to write it and then giving up after a paragraph or two and going out to play ball. Also, in those days there was a lot of radio drama, afternoon and evening, always with introductory music to set the mood. And so I'd get a vague inspiration of one sort or another and then put a record on the phonograph, some music I felt was dramatic, an opera overture, a jazz tune, and imagine it as the beginning of a scene or episode for a radio story that was going to come to me at any minute.

It is possible that my writing clock had been set back by the seismic shock of puberty, a whole new way of thinking or obsessing that only tied in with the idea of writing on such occasions as my discovery of *Mademoiselle de Maupin* by Théophile Gautier, a racy French novel that, as I read it even in circumspect translation, made my heart pound and my ears turn red. Around this time the war ended, my brother came home unscathed, and he resumed his undergraduate career at City College, today known as CUNY, where he enrolled in a writing class and proceeded to write a novel during the course of a winter on his portable typewriter each night at the kitchen table. It told of the peacetime adjustment problems of some army veterans returning to their old neighborhoods. This in fact is what all the postwar novels seemed to be about, and my brother subsequently abandoned his effort. But seeing him tapping away late into the night had its effect on me. Here was our own family war hero proposing the act of writing as the serious endeavor of a responsible adult, the pages accumulating right before my eyes.

A year or so later I found myself a student at the Bronx High School of Science, an institution filled with insufferably brilliant children, some of whom were quite convinced, correctly as it turned out, that they would in time win the Nobel Prize in physics. Meanwhile, instead of doing the assigned lab work, I was reading Kafka's stories, *Metamorphosis* and the rest, and hanging out with the other displaced humanists in a little corner office where *Dynamo*, the school's literary magazine, was published. Inevitably it published something of mine, a short story entitled "The Beetle," my teenage homage to the master's really cool use of entomological self-defamation. But that was hardly enough to satisfy what was now almost a physical need to write, and so when I had the opportunity to enroll in a journalism class for the usual English course credit, I jumped at it.

There are, to tell the truth, fewer epiphanies in life than there are in literature—I mean in the Joycean sense of the term, those moments of inexorable moral definition that predict a life, a fate. I suppose I am fortunate to be able to identify one, retrospec-

tively, in my life. What happened was this: our high school journalism teacher ordered us to go out into the world and conduct
an interview. I threw myself into the assignment, exercising ini-
tiative, working hard, and I turned in an interview with the stage
doorman at Carnegie Hall. He was a German Jewish refugee,
a camp survivor, the only one in his family, a prematurely aged
sweet-tempered man with rheumy eyes, who wore an old double-
breasted blue serge jacket, unbuttoned, and baggy brown pants.
Each evening he came to work with his lunch in a paper bag and
a thermos of hot tea. He drank his tea in the old-world way by
putting a cube of sugar between his teeth and sipping the tea
through the sugar. His life had been shattered but he had spirit,
and he knew the repertoire, he could speak knowledgeably about
composers and musicians. Over the years he'd become a fixture
in the place, and all the great recitalists, Horowitz, Rubinstein,
Jascha Heifetz, knew him and called him by his first name, Karl.
Karl the Doorman.

My teacher was so impressed with the piece that she decided
it should run in the school newspaper. She called me up to her
front desk after class and said she wanted one of the photography
students to go down to Carnegie Hall and take the old doorman's
picture to go along with the story. I had not anticipated this degree
of enthusiasm. I said I didn't think that was possible—Karl would
never let his picture be taken.

"Why?" she asked.

"Well, he's very shy."

"How shy can he be?" she said. "He talked to you, didn't he?"

"Well not exactly," I said. "There is no Karl the Doorman. I
made him up."

Once more in my child's life, I had yielded the high ground
to the other life form. My teacher would bring up the big guns, a

trip to the principal's office, a note to my parents, before she was through. But it had seemed to me so much better to make up that stage doorman than actually to go through the tedious business of interviewing someone. If there wasn't a Karl the Doorman, there should have been. And what about Kafka, after all, he wrote from his imagination about things that weren't verifiable from the real everyday world, but they were true!

Not that I tried to defend myself. Today I would of course explain to the teacher that I had done no more than what journalists have always done.

But I have since thought about this incident. It is, I suppose, a novelist's story. It can stand as a kind of parable of the novelist's birth. For the practice has taught me that nothing I write will turn out well unless during the course of the writing I feel the same thrill of transgression I felt as I put together from my young life and times the images I needed for the invention of Karl the Stage Doorman at Carnegie Hall. I believe nothing of any beauty or truth comes of a piece of writing without the author's thinking he has sinned against something—propriety, custom, faith, privacy, tradition, political orthodoxy, historical fact, literary convention, or indeed, all the prevailing community standards together. And that the work will not be realized without the liberation that comes to the writer from his feeling of having transgressed, broken the rules, played a forbidden game—without his understanding or even fearing his work as a possibly unforgivable transgression.

Karl, of course, was of the same profession as the forbidding-looking guard in Kafka's *The Trial*, who stands at the door to The Law and who tells the poor supplicant at the end of his life that the door had been his to pass through had he tried. My doorman Karl stood at the door to The Music and addressed me unambiguously in my teen age and I thank God for him.

"Open it," he told me. "Go ahead, my boy, this door is intended for you. It's your door to open. Open it."

Finding the Known World

EDWARD P. JONES

April 21, 2005

The Known World began with an image of a dying man. It came to me sometime in 1991 or '92, not long after I had completed my first book. The completion of a book of fiction, I have discovered now for the second time, leaves a kind of creative emptiness. And the hungry mind begins searching the universe of what you know and what you can imagine for something to fill that emptiness. And it so happened that about this time I recalled one small fact from my early years at Holy Cross College. This fact, as I remember, stood alone, a one-line footnote in a book or maybe even a passing comment by a professor. The fact was that there had been black slave owners in America. There was no background to that fact, no book about it or even a chapter in a book, no full-period lecture by a professor. Just that one plain-and-simple fact, that once upon a time there had been black people in America who had owned their own kind.

I began, then, to think I might want to write a novel about that world, of a people who chose to participate in a system that oppressed their own. Before college, when I was about sixteen or seventeen, I read a rather thin paperback book about an American Jew who, having fallen far off the track that was his proper and good life, joined the American Nazi party without, of course, divulging his identity. I had been fascinated, to be sure, that someone would choose to throw in with people who, if they had their way, would annihilate him and his people. I don't remember the man's name or all that happened to him. I do recall feeling a sadness about the whole matter, and I felt somewhat the same when I discovered that there had been black slave owners.

So this hungry mind set out to write a first novel. What I knew about slavery in the United States is what the average educated American knows, I suppose. Some of it comes from books, and some—perhaps too much—comes from movies and television. I did know enough about myself and what stands as good writing to know that what I knew would not be enough for a novel that might run three hundred pages or more. So I set out to educate myself about slavery. I already had about thirty books on the subject, and I bought some dozen more. The books covered a variety of subjects: family life and slavery, slave revolts, the economics of slavery, and narratives collected from former slaves during the Great Depression. There were also three or four books on black slave owners, books I bought sometime in the 1980s, long before the idea of a novel came to me.

I don't remember the first book I started in on, but I found it all rather uninspiring. I believe that was because I was reading not for simple edification, and certainly not for the old-fashioned, pure pleasure of reading. The reading was simply a means to begin building a novel. I had a goal—that of writing the novel—and to get there I had to go through this forest of reading. My heart was not in it. After about thirty pages or so, I stopped. I did manage to take several pages of notes, facts about what work slaves did beyond toiling in the field—blacksmiths, seamstresses, carpenters, etc. But I had no heart for any more reading and put the notes away and returned the book to the shelf.

Periodically over the next several years—beginning in '93 and '94—I would go back to the bookshelf. I never again picked up that first book, but chose another: *The Negro in Virginia*, a book on slavery in that commonwealth, put together by people in the Works Progress Administration. But I never finished that book either, for the same reason. I had no heart for all that research. This is all very curious to me, because I'm not a person who sits around and contemplates himself. But year after year—and it happened for maybe five or six years—I would take this book, *The Negro in Virginia*, down, get through the first forty pages, and just stop. I never took any notes—I'm not sure why—and I would put the book away. And the next year, because I hadn't taken any notes, I had to read the same pages again. I would get to about the same point and I would stop, put the book back on the shelf, and the next year I would do the same thing. I do remember those forty pages. They contained, I think, two facts that I ended up putting in my book. One was that in 1806, the state of Virginia passed a law that said all freed slaves had about a year to get out of the state unless some white benefactor appealed to the legislature. And I also came across in those forty pages the fact that—I think in the first or second year, when the law was still fresh—exceptions were made for a black barber and a black baker, both of whom had mostly white customers.

This is all the research I did for *The Known World*—those first pages from *The Negro in Virginia*. This is all the research from that first thought, in '91 or '92, about the dying man until I sat down to write the novel in earnest in 2001. I never went back to those pages of notes from the very first book. By the time I got down to writing, I did not want to decipher notes from nearly ten years before. Some of those notes, I concluded, might not even make sense now that I was no longer the man who had written them. And of course, I never got around to reading any of the other books. I'm not altogether certain why I felt no excitement about doing the research. It might be that at heart I am a fiction writer, not a historian. The facts I need are in the imagination. The facts and the truth of a world are what I make up.

One strange thing—perhaps the strangest—is that while I spent some ten years avoiding all that research—all those forty or more books—the creative part of me was working away, month after month, year after year. That hungry mind that needed to create used the seed of the image of the dying man, of Henry Townsend, and went on without me, the person who did not write because he felt he first needed to read those books. In my imagination I saw Henry Townsend as the owner of some thirty-three human beings. He is a black man, and he's lying on his deathbed. He is thirty-one years old, young even for the American year I was going to put him in: 1855. In the room with him are three women, and the job the creative part of my brain had for itself was to show over the next three-hundred-plus pages how the four came to be in that room. It was, of course, not an easy job, but it was far easier—and far more pleasurable—than reading forty books.

I don't really have people I share my work with, but in those first weeks of writing, a friend of mine who is a great reader of books and knows literature when she sees it wanted to know what I was doing. So I gave her the first ten pages or so, including the section in which Henry is dying and in the room is his wife, Caldonia, and their teacher, Fern. In the moments as Henry is dying, Fern and Caldonia are discussing a Thomas Gray poem, "Elegy Written in a Country Churchyard," which is one I came across when I was a freshman at Holy Cross. I think this discussion between Fern and Caldonia went on for about two paragraphs or so. It wasn't very long. Anyway, my friend Marcia came back to me and she didn't have a great many comments to make, but one thing she did say was, "Well, it all sounded rather highfalutin." And I didn't think so, but I agreed that I had to do something about that, so I changed it. I took out all the stuff about the poem, and I put the paragraph below in instead. And this ended up to be very good, because in the paragraph there is a kind of switch in terms of who is a slave and who is not a slave, and in a certain way it became the theme for the entire book.

It was several minutes before Caldonia and Fern knew Henry was no more and they went on talking about a widowed white woman with two slaves to her name on a farm in some distant part of Virginia, in a place near Montross where her nearest white neighbors were miles and miles away. The news of the young woman, Elizabeth Marson, was more than one year old, but it was only now reaching the people of Manchester County, so the women in the room with dead Henry spoke as if it had all happened to Elizabeth just that morning. After the white woman's husband died, her slaves, Mirtha and Destiny, had taken over and kept the woman prisoner for months, working her ragged with only a few hours rest each day until her hair turned white and her pores sweated blood. Caldonia said she understood that Mirtha and Destiny had been sold to try to compensate Elizabeth, to settle her away from that farm with its memories, but Fern said she understood that the slave women had been killed by the law. When Elizabeth was finally rescued, she did not remember that she was supposed to be the owner of those slaves, and it was a long time before she could be taught that again. Caldonia, noticing her husband's stillness, went to him. She gave a cry as she shook him. Loretta, the maid, came in silently and took a hand mirror from atop the dresser. It seemed to Caldonia as she watched Loretta place the mirror under Henry's nose that he had only stepped away and that if she called loudly enough to him, put her mouth close to his ear and called loud enough for any slave in the quarters to hear, he might turn back and be her husband again. She took Henry's hand in both of hers and put it to her cheek. It was warm, she noticed, thinking there might be yet enough life in him for him to reconsider.

Now, that section, while it was written in my head, was years and years away from being put down on paper or on a computer page that anyone could read. I felt I did not deserve to physically write even one word of the book until I had done all the homework, all the research. I did manage in those ten years to treat myself to twelve pages of writing on the computer. I believe the writing of those pages was born of a need to actually see something physical, in black and white, on the page. But those twelve pages were all. They were six pages of the opening chapter, leading up to Henry Townsend dying, and six pages of the final chapter. I didn't write anything else but those twelve pages, not even one line on a three-by-five card. But the creative part of my mind worked away and was able to hold more than 370 pages of the novel, which eventually became 388 pages. Not everything in my head was written in detail—much of it was scrawled across my brain in a very general way. And it was scrawled as I waited for the bus or the

subway. It was scrawled as I shopped up and down the aisles of the
Safeway. It was even scrawled as I read the *New York Times* or
watched television.

So after ten years, it came to be Christmas 2001. I was then
working from home at a nowhere job, for Tax Analysts and several of its publications. I was summarizing newspaper and magazine articles, op-eds, editorials, and columns on federal and state
taxes and tax-exempt organizations. I was becoming unhappy that
so much time—ten years—so much of my life had gone by, and I
had only those twelve pages to show for it. I didn't count the work
that was in my head—it was real; it was there—but it wasn't something I could hold in my hand and perhaps show the world, if the
world ever came calling. I had about eight weeks of vacation time
from my day job, and I decided to take five weeks and really dig
into the research.

I began on Christmas, which I think was a Monday that year.
I was in earnest; I was determined. There were two shelves of
books—forty books—and I knew that I could spend five weeks
of vacation reading maybe fifteen or so books, and I still wouldn't
be anywhere near to writing the novel. It occurred to me that if I
was to make use of the vacation time, I should simply start writing some of what was in my head. Those six pages of that first
chapter gave me a good head start, and by the eighth of January,
2002, I had written into physical form about seventy-five pages
of *The Known World*. The eighth of January is important because
that afternoon a guy from my day job called me at home, on vacation, and told me that I didn't have a job anymore. I was less than
a month shy of having been there nineteen years. They gave me
two months' severance for the nineteen years. The day job had
given me the used computer on which I was writing the novel,
and before they would give me any severance, I had to promise to

return the computer and not to sue them. I waited until the very last day to agree. Over nearly two weeks of writing, from the first days after Christmas until the eighth of January, I had developed a relationship with the computer. I got up each morning, turned on the computer, and it never failed to show me all the work I had done the day before. And it never failed to allow me to complete the five more pages I set as my goal each day. I am not a computer person, and I was terrified at the thought of having to give up the machine, to learn to work on something else. Which is why I waited until the very last day to send the form agreeing to their terms for severance pay. In the end, they never came for the computer, and they sent the two months' severance. I struggled on and managed to finish the first draft of the novel by about mid-March, less than three months after I began.

Because I'm not the kind of person who sits around and thinks about himself, I'm starting to learn things just by way of the questions that come at me. About a month ago, I had been on the road and I returned home. It was Thursday, it was about eight o'clock, and all I wanted to do was plop down on the floor. I had moved back to Washington. I'd had furniture when I moved, but it was twenty-one years old, so I'd thrown it away. I don't have a car, and I don't have a lot of time, so I hadn't been able to get furniture, and I was sleeping on the floor. People always ask me, "All these prizes and everything, have they changed your life?" Well, if my life had been changed, I wouldn't be sleeping on the floor.

The phone rang—and I suppose you have that problem too, people calling and trying to sell you stuff. I lived in a ninth-floor apartment for twenty-one years in Arlington, Virginia, and every now and again somebody would call and ask if I wanted to hire them to sweep my chimney. So the phone rang and this woman said, "Is this Edward Jones?"

And I said, "Is this a telemarketer?"

And she said, "No, it's Oprah Winfrey."

So. It wasn't a secretary—it was her; I guess she dialed the number herself. And we proceeded to have a conversation for about thirty-five minutes. Mostly what she wanted to know was what was real and what was not real in the novel—and, question after question, I just kept saying, "I made it all up. I made it all up."

But after we had spoken, and after I had gone out on the road again, about two weeks later, I began to realize that the ten years of thinking this novel through was probably what saved me after they took my job away. When you grow up in certain circumstances, a job is very important for you; it sort of holds you to the world, holds you to the rest of humanity. And when you don't have a job, you feel as if you're floating out there alone, without any kind of support. I think now that if I had not had this whole novel written out, mostly in a general way in my head, I would have gotten up on Wednesday—the guy called me on Tuesday—in a very depressed state. But I had a plan—a ten-year plan in my head—and on Wednesday I was still hurting, I felt very bad, but I got up, turned on the computer, and I did the five or so pages again. For most of the rest of January, I kept writing. Sometimes it was even more than five pages. I have a calendar where I kept note of my progress, the pages I did each day, and it was only toward the end of January that there were days when I did no work. And it wasn't really related to not having the job—there are some days, even when you have a plan, when the mind doesn't respond.

I was never certain of what I had written. I was never certain of what I had. I had written a book with no reader in mind other than myself. I had always believed that you cannot write with any faith in yourself when you write according to what some reader in Dubuque or Albuquerque might like. The reader I tried to satisfy, day after day, was me. But who was I to say whether what I had produced was any good? We are all, in the end, capable of bad taste at any time. Especially when the dominant voice we hear is the one in our head. As I wrote the book, I was guided, for the most part, by two things: the unadorned poetry of the Bible and the sound of my mother speaking. I had gone to graduate school at the University of Virginia at a time when I had published only one short story. While working toward a master of fine arts degree in creative writing, I was fortunate to take one academic course that I perhaps treasure more than all my other courses. It was the Bible as Literature, given by Dr. Neurenberger. I had never read anything but snippets of the Bible. I had never sat down and actually read it from cover to cover. The course not only introduced me to the people and stories in the work but it also showed me a poetic and reportorial mode of writing. The Jerusalem Bible, which is far from the stiffness of the King James version, offers writing about horrendous events that isn't cluttered with the kind of emotional language that begs the reader to feel but rarely to think. The story of a people is tragic in itself, and the telling of that story will produce the emotion on its own for any reader with a heart. I can still remember coming upon the moment in the Jerusalem Bible when they throw the prophet Jeremiah down a well. There was very little beyond the reporting of the facts of the situation, the facts about the man. But I had come to know Jeremiah, come to know what he was trying to do, and that report of him being tossed down the well grabbed and touched me.

The other voice guiding me as I wrote was that of my mother. I had grown up hearing her speak with a certain cadence, a cadence born of the South. Southern people come into the world knowing how to tell a story, and they tell it with a language that is often poetic, a language of stories within stories. A Southerner cannot tell you a simple story of a family moving from one place to another on a straight road without informing you about each world the family moves through as they make their way. *Now this Smith family, this poor Smith family, with them two murder-in-the-eyes children, got to the place where the old Sawmill Road juts right past the road they call "The Bowlegged Woman with a Dead Husband Road." Lemme tell you how it got that name. And you remind me to get back to the Smith family with them two murder-in-the-eyes children if I forget.* My mother's language was full of colorful little sayings, morals, lessons: "Each shut-eye ain't sleep." "Every goodbye ain't gone." "A good run beats a bad stand any day." "Some families live long lives, but when they go out, they go out like popcorn, one after the other."

My mother also had a number of superstitions. I remember vividly that whenever she'd comb or brush her hair, she would take the hair out of the comb and brush, put it in the ashtray—she was a smoker, which is what led to her death in the end—and burn the hair. She believed that if the hair ended up in the trash, birds would get it somehow and that she would be plagued with headaches forever after. I was about three or four when, I remember, we were walking down Fourth Street, and she pointed to a spot on the street and she said some man had been killed there; I think he had been shot. It was a sunny day, and she said, "Well, if you ever come by this way and it's raining, you'll be able to see the man's blood." I never got around to doing that—I wasn't really interested in seeing that man's blood. But that was her belief, that even decades and decades after someone had died violently, you could go there in the rain, and the rain would show the blood.

With all of that, then, it was easy and natural for me to imagine, as I do in the novel, a street in the fictional town of Manchester where three boys burst into flames for no other reason than that the universe is a weird place. In a novel, I can imagine lightning snaking along the ground, moving about as if it has a mind, choosing to kill birds and trees, but also choosing to run away from a man intent on ending his own life. So it was with the two voices—the biblical and my mother's—that I wrote *The Known World.* I should say that in addition to not reading those forty or so books on slavery, I also never got around to visiting a friend in Lynchburg, Virginia, and using his county as a setting for the novel. I had thought he and I would travel his county in his pickup truck, and I would take notes and go home and inhabit that real world around Lynchburg with the imaginary people I had created. But visiting my friend was something else I never got around to doing. So in those first days after Christmas 2001, when I began writing, I was forced out of necessity to create my own county. I decided to call it "Manchester" because that had a nice British ring to it. I placed my unreal Manchester County in an area just south of Charlottesville, where I'd gone to school, and just north of Lynchburg, where my friend lives. I called Manchester "the largest county in Virginia," because the book in my head had dozens upon dozens of characters, and a thousand and one things were happening in it. I surrounded Manchester with real Virginia counties, because I wanted readers to leave the novel believing that Manchester and its people had existed, once upon a time. For that same reason, I invented a multitude of facts about Manchester, such as those in the following paragraph:

The 1840 U.S. Census contained an enormous amount of facts, far more than the one done by the alcoholic state delegate in 1830, and all of the 1840 census facts pointed to the one big fact that Manchester was then the largest county in Virginia, a place of 2,191 slaves, 142 free Negroes, 939 whites, and 136 Indians, most of them Cherokee but with a sprinkling of Choctaw. A well-liked and fastidious tanner, who doubled as the U.S. marshal and who had lost three fingers to frostbite, carried out the 1840 census in seven and a half summer weeks. It should have taken him less time but he had plenty of trouble, starting with people like Harvey Travis who wanted to make sure his own children were counted as white, though all the world knew his wife was a full-blooded Cherokee. Travis even called his children niggers and filthy half-breeds when they and that world got to be too much for him. The census taker/tanner/U.S. marshal told Travis he would count the children as white but he actually wrote in his report to the federal government in Washington, D.C., that they were slaves, the property of their father, which, in the eyes of the law, they truly were; the census taker had never seen the children before the day he rode out to Travis's place on one of two mules the American government had bought for him so he could do his census job. He thought the children were too dark for him and the federal government to consider them as anything else but black. He told his government the children were slaves and he let it go at that, not saying anything about their white blood or their Indian blood. The census taker had a great belief that his government could read between the lines. And though he came away with suspicions about Travis's wife being a full Indian, he gave Travis the benefit of the doubt and listed her as "American Indian/Full Cherokee." The census taker also had trouble trying to calculate how many square miles the county was, and in the end he sent in figures that were far short of the mark. The mountains, he told a confidant, threw him off because he was unable to take the measure of the land with the damn mountains in the way.

Now, I've had a number of people come up to me and tell me that they believe the place is real, that Manchester County is a real place. How could it not be real if I have all those census figures? And I'm not sure why, but it seems as if it's too great a leap for a lot of people to believe that you can simply come up with numbers. There's also, in the novel, a Canadian who comes to America in the 1870s and makes a living writing pamphlets. I was interviewed by a *Washington Post* reporter who said he had looked on the Internet for this man, Anderson Frazier. After the novel was finished, my editor suggested that we put a few lines inside—maybe on the opposite of the title page—saying that none of the characters were real, that they were not based on any real people. And I told her, and I tell other people, that there shouldn't be any need for that because on the front of the book it says, "a novel."

The fact that I did not do any research, that I did not use my friend's county as a setting for the novel, may well have worked to my benefit. Had I read all those books, I would have come upon a million facts about slavery that I would have been tempted to use. The result could have been a novel in which all those wonderful facts dominated, and the characters I had imagined would have been pushed to the background. One of the books that I never got around to reading—it has nice pictures in it; when I bought it, it had this cellophane wrapping on it, and I did unwrap it and flip through it and there are nice pictures of houses and everything— was about the architecture of the nineteenth century: what went into building a mansion, and even what went into building a slave cabin. And this is one of those things that, again, has sort of come to me in the course of being asked questions. But, I mean, I could have read all that about what goes into making a slave cabin, and I would have been able to maybe have a whole page of all that goes into it.

Now, in the novel, in the first pages there is a slave, Elias, and it's about nine at night, dark. He's sitting on a tree stump, and the only light he has is a very feeble lantern behind him, over near the door of his cabin. He's whittling a doll for his daughter. And I talk about him in the moments when I'm writing about his carving a doll, as well as later on, but I think when I'm talking about him carving a doll is the reader's first introduction to Elias. And one of the things I'm realizing is that if I'd put all that stuff about what goes into building a slave cabin, and then introduced Elias, all the facts would have had to share the same page or pages, and Elias might have gotten lost. I think I'm realizing that *my* job—as this writer, as this creator of Elias—is to present the man in the very best way that I can and that the intelligent reader can build his or her own cabin.

Had I visited my friend in Lynchburg and adopted that area as a setting for the book, I might also have had the problem that every fact I used about the real place might have been scrutinized by diligent readers who know the history of the place. Such readers live to call you on your mistakes. In creating my own imaginary place, I could say whatever I wanted about Manchester County and its people and its history. I could make up census records about it, and in the end I could tear the county asunder, which is what I did.

Some have asked if the novel that was in my head all that time is what finally ended up on the page. For the most part, what is there between the covers of the book is essentially what I had mapped out in my head. There were only a few surprises. In some cases, a story I'd created could not fit into the house that I began building when I was writing. Elias is married to Celeste, who is also a slave, of course, and she's crippled. Over those ten years, I had worked out a small story about Celeste and her grandfather, who go out in the rain one day because they have this yearning for blueberries. In the novel as it is now, I say that Celeste was born crippled. But in this story, she wasn't born crippled. She's about eight or nine and they go out in the rain and then there's thunder and lightning, and at one point a bolt of lightning comes down to the ground and runs along the ground. I had this nice phrase: "It was running like a snake with feet." The bolt of lightning kills the grandfather. But before he dies, he turns to his granddaughter Celeste and tells her to run. She starts running. And the lightning—in another phrase: "The lightning, still hungry"—runs after Celeste, grabs her leg, and twists it, and that's how she becomes crippled.

I think that's the strange thing, that what you write in your mind is not quite always the same thing as what you can see on the page. And the story about Celeste being crippled has to come in the first part of the book, when all the people are being introduced; it would not work in the second section. But in all those early chapters, I could not find a place for that story. There is a very long chapter—the longest, I think—that has to do with Elias and Celeste coming together and his attempt, before that, to run away. And I could not put the story in there without unbalancing that chapter. The same thing with all the other chapters. So I didn't use it. Once Dawn Davis, the woman who became my editor, read the manuscript and sent it back, she had very few suggestions and comments. And I think she called it at one point "a clean manuscript," and I think that's what happens when you work on something for ten years in your head.

There's also a slave called Stanford in the book. He was a man who spent his entire life chasing after young women, and there comes a point in 1855 when those women are no longer attracted to him, he's full of bad liquor, and he decides that he is going to commit suicide. He's going out into the field to find a place to do this, and just before he does, he sees two kids in the rain, going to get blueberries. And he decides, *Well, I'm gonna kill myself, maybe if I get these kids some blueberries God will let me into heaven.* Originally, Stanford was just beaten up, nursed back to health, and then he went on with his life. But once Dawn sent the manuscript back to me, I remembered that whole story about the blueberries and the rain, and I decided to use it; it's what's in the novel now. One thing I've learned about myself as a writer is that even if I don't use a story line right away, I'll find a use for it somewhere down the line.

Another surprise, as I pulled the novel out of my head, involved some minor people. I had always intended that the sheriff of Manchester County, John Skiffington, be a minor character who takes on a prominent role only at the end. But as I was writing, Skiffington became more and more important. I found that I could not tell the story of that county without putting the sheriff at the center of what was happening. The same thing occurred with the richest white man in Manchester County, William Robbins. I saw that I had to bring Robbins nearer and nearer to the center of the stage, or I couldn't do what I needed to do. Along the way, some characters disappeared altogether, because the novel could not sustain them. An insane white lawyer, for example, who abhors slavery but befriends and aids the black slave owner Henry Townsend. There was also a freed slave who was cast out into the world with nothing but a horse that is destined to be killed only hours after the man achieves freedom.

It was really a nice story about this man. I mean, you shouldn't praise your own poem, but sometimes you can't help it. And it would have run, I think, six or seven pages. He gets out there and he's on this horse and it's the only possession he has, he's newly freed, and the only thing he owns in the world is this horse, and the horse steps into a hole and breaks its leg. A man who looks white comes along and tells him, "Well, you've got a bit of bad luck there." The man pulls out a gun and says, "Do you want me to do this?" And the freed slave says yes, and the man shoots the horse in the head. I've noticed in the novel that a lot of horses get shot in the head. There are two that I'm thinking about right now. I have nothing against horses; I just had to tell my story. But anyway, this freed slave and this man become friends, and the man takes him home, and they live together for years and years in a nice and happy life. But again, while the story was written in my head and where I wanted to put it made sense, once I started writing, I couldn't find a place for it without unbalancing the chapters.

One other surprise, one that played itself out over ten years, is how the book expanded beyond my original intent. While the first image I may have had was that of Henry Townsend dying, I'd always thought that I would concentrate almost exclusively on the slaves that Henry owned, some thirty-three human beings. They were to live in what I was going to call "The Village," a complex of sixteen cabins, eight on one side of a lane and eight on the other. I wanted to present in that village as wide, colorful, and profound a variety of people as I could imagine. I was interested in their masters—Henry and his wife, Caldonia—and in all the people in Manchester County, but only so far as they could help me tell the story of those thirty-three slaves.

In the beginning, because I was just going to write about those slaves, I planned to title the novel *All Aunt Hagar's Children*. "Aunt Hagar's children" is a phrase my mother used for black people. But once I got into the writing of it and, as I said, people, especially white people, took on greater roles—Skiffington and William Robbins—I realized that I would have to come up with a title that encompassed all of that. And it just so happened that a few years before I had started writing, the Library of Congress had bought a map that is said to be the first on which the word "America" ever appeared. I didn't know I was going to use that, but I tore the article out of the newspaper. When I got to a point, in chapter five, where Skiffington is at his jail, I decided right then to have that map on his wall. In the article, there's not a lot of information about the map, so what's in the novel is mostly just made up. And of course the legend is my own making as well: *The Known World*.

But I suppose that just as the creative part of the mind can't be held back by the more orderly part of the mind that believes it needs to do research first, it can't be confined once creativity begins. The more I tried to stay only in that village of sixteen cabins over those ten years of thinking, the more I sometimes wandered away—up to the giant house where Henry and Caldonia lived, and up and down the roads of Manchester County.

Most of the events in *The Known World* occur in 1855. I began writing the novel nearly 150 years later, when, to be sure, all the characters would have been dead. So much, I believe, would have been different for me as a writer if I had been writing in 1870, some fifteen years after the events, or even in 1900. Writing so soon after 1855 would have made me a kind of contemporary of those characters, who might still have been living, even if only in my imagination. But writing in 2001 and 2002, I became—and I do not say this in any grandiose way, but rather as a simple storyteller responsible for all the people I imagined—the god of the world I was creating. Every character would be dead, and that meant I knew not only the moment they came into the world but also when and how they left the world. And, as the god of that place—that imaginary place—I sometimes found a need, as I was writing about people, to pause and tell the story of what happened to them after 1855. The characters' lives are all of one piece; the people in the novel might not be able to remember some event of their childhood that would have meaning when they were much, much older. Characters might not see how their lives are one piece, but their creator can. And sometimes the creator needs to stop and show how that childhood event comes back.

The best example of this is with Elias and that doll he fashions for his daughter. He's making the doll in about July of 1855. Several months later the doll is finished, and his daughter Tessie is walking the lane. There are visitors in the lane, one of them comments on the doll, and Tessie says, "My daddy made it for me." I don't remember what it was in me at that moment when she says that, but I found myself needing to stop and jump ahead ninety years to a moment when Tessie is on her deathbed. And it comes into her mind to say, "My daddy made it for me," and she asks her family to find the doll, so they find it in the attic and bring it down to her. Tessie wouldn't have remembered that she had spoken the words at six years old. I have to remember for her, and for the reader. I don't think I could have done that if I were writing about the daughter only fifteen years after she had turned six. That would have been science fiction, which I cannot do. Imaginary history is a different matter.

I suppose it is inevitable that a black person writing about slavery leads to speculation that the writer has some agenda. I know that that is not true about me. I had no agenda; I had no issues I wanted to present. I always felt, from the first words to the last words, that I was telling a simple story about complex people who usually tried to do the best they could but who often came up short. Had I set out with some agenda, I'd have had to slight some characters, present them as either all of one thing or all of another, good or bad, as it were. I could not have shown some characters in all their complexity. An agenda—propaganda—rarely allows for that. People are all things on all days.

"Where Do You Get Your Ideas From?"

URSULA K. LE GUIN

October 11, 2000

"Where do you get your ideas from?" is the question people in my line of work—fiction writers—get asked most often. We never know how to answer. In self-defense, most of us develop a sound-bite answer. Harlan Ellison's is the best; he says he gets his ideas from a mail-order house in Schenectady.

When people ask, "Where do you get your ideas from?" what some of them really want to know is the address of that mail-order company.

That is, they want to write, or more likely what they want is to be a writer, because they know writers are rich and famous; and they know that there are secrets that writers know, like that address in Schenectady; and they know that if they can just learn those secrets, those mystical post-office box numbers, they will be Stephen King.

Alas. Writers don't have secrets. Except maybe the well-kept secret that about 99 percent of writers are neither rich nor famous. Writers talk. Writers are wordy people. They talk, blab, whine all the time to each other about what they're writing; they teach writing workshops and write writing books and yadder on talk shows. Writers tell all. If they could tell beginning writers where to get ideas, they would. In fact they do, all the time. Some of them actually get rich and famous by doing it.

What do the how-to-write writers say about getting ideas? They say stuff like: "Listen to conversations, note down interesting things you hear or read about, keep a journal, describe a character, imagine a dresser drawer and describe what's in it"—yeah, yeah, but that's all work. Anybody can do work. I wanna be a writer. What's the PO box number?

Well, the secret to writing is writing. Writing is how you be a writer. It's only a secret to people who really don't want to hear it.

So why do I want to try to answer this foolish question, "Where do you get your ideas from?" Because underneath the foolish aspect of it, the question is a real one that people really want to know the answer to, even though it is ultimately unanswerable; and unanswerable questions are just what fiction writers like to answer.

It's a big question—where do writers get their ideas, where do artists get their visions, where do musicians get their music? It's bound to have a big answer. Or a whole lot of them.

One of my favorite answers is this: Somebody asked Willie Nelson how he thought up his tunes, and he said, "The air is full of tunes, I just reach up and pick one."

Now that is not a secret. But it is a sweet mystery.

And a true one. For a fiction writer—a storyteller—the world is full of stories, and when a story is there, it's there; you just reach up and pick it.

Then you have to be able to let it tell itself.

First you have to be able to wait. To wait in silence. Wait in silence and listen. Listen for the tune, the vision, the story. Not grabbing, not pushing, just waiting, listening, being ready for it when it comes. This is an act of trust. Trust in yourself, trust in the world. The artist says, "The world will give me what I need and I will be able to use it rightly."

Readiness—not grabbiness, not greed—readiness: willingness to hear, to listen carefully, to see clearly and accurately—to let the words be right. Not almost right. Right. To know how to make something out of the vision; that's what practice is for. Because being ready doesn't mean just sitting around, even if it looks like that's what writers mostly do; artists practice their art continually, and writing happens to involve a lot of sitting. Scales and finger exercises, pencil sketches, endless unfinished and rejected stories. The artist who practices knows the difference between practice and performance, and the essential connection between them. The gift of those seemingly wasted hours and years is patience and readiness; a good ear, a keen eye, and a skilled hand, a rich vocabulary and grammar. The gift of practice to the artist is mastery, or a word I like better, "craft."

With those tools, those instruments, with that hard-earned mastery, that craftiness, you do your best to let the "idea"—the tune, the vision, the story—come through clear and undistorted. Clear of ineptitude, awkwardness, amateurishness; undistorted by convention, fashion, opinion.

This is a very radical job, dealing with the ideas you get if you are an artist and take your job seriously, this shaping a vision into the medium of words. It's what I like best to do in the world, and what I like to talk about when I talk about writing. I could happily go on and on about it. But I'm trying to talk about where the vision, the stuff you work on, the "idea," comes from. So:

The air is full of tunes.

A piece of rock is full of statues.

The earth is full of visions.

The world is full of stories.

As an artist, you trust that. You trust that that is so. You know it is so. You know that whatever your experience, it will give you the material, the "ideas," for your work. (From here on I'll leave out music and fine arts and stick to storytelling, which is the only thing I truly know anything about, though I do think all the arts are one at the root.)

"Idea"—what does that word mean? "Idea" is shorthand for the material, the subject, subjects, the matter of a story. What the story is about. What the story *is*. "Idea" is a strange word for an imagined matter, not abstract but intensely concrete, not intellectual but embodied. However, "idea" is the word we're stuck with. And it's not wholly off center, because the imagination is a rational faculty.

"I got the idea for that story from a dream I had."

"I haven't had a good story idea all year."

"Here am I sitting after half the morning, crammed with ideas, and visions, and so on, and can't dislodge them, for lack of the right rhythm."

That last sentence was written in 1926 by Virginia Woolf, in a letter to a writer friend. I will come back to it in the end, because what she says about rhythm goes deeper than anything I have ever thought or read about where art comes from. But before I can talk about rhythm I have to talk about experience and imagination.

Where do writers get their ideas from? From experience. That's obvious.

And from imagination. That's less obvious.

Fiction results from imagination working on experience. We shape experience in our minds so that it makes sense. We force the world to be coherent, to tell us a story.

Not only fiction writers do this; we all do it; we do it constantly, in order to survive. People who can't make the world into a story, go mad. Or, like infants or (perhaps) animals, they live in a world that has no history, no time but now.

The minds of animals are a great, sacred, present mystery. I do think animals have languages, but they are entirely truthful languages. It seems that we are the only animals who can *lie*—who can think and say what is not so and never was so, or what has never been yet might be. We can invent; we can suppose; we can imagine. All that gets mixed in with memory. And so we're the only animals who can tell stories.

An ape can extrapolate from her experience: once I stuck a stick in that anthill and the ants crawled on it, and so if I put this stick in that anthill again, maybe the ants will crawl on it again and I can lick them off again, yum. But only we human beings can imagine—can tell the story about the ape who stuck a stick in an anthill and it came out covered with gold dust and a prospector saw it and that was the beginning of the great gold rush of 1877 in Rhodesia.

That story is not true. It is fiction. Its only relation to reality is the fact that some apes do stick sticks in anthills. There was no gold rush in 1877 in Rhodesia. I made it up. I am a human; therefore I lie. All humans are liars; that is true—you must believe me.

Fiction: Imagination working on experience. A great deal of what we consider our experience, our memory, our hard-earned knowledge, our history, is in fact fiction. But never mind that; I'm talking about real fiction, stories, novels. They all come from the writer's experience of reality worked upon, changed, filtered, distorted, clarified, transfigured, by imagination.

"Ideas" come from the world through the head.

The interesting part of this process, to me, is the passage through the head, the action of the imagination on the raw material. But that's the part of the process that a great many people disapprove of.

I wrote a piece years ago called "Why Are Americans Afraid of Dragons?" In it I talked about how so many Americans distrust and despise not only the obviously imaginative kind of fiction we call fantasy, but also all fiction, often rationalizing their fear and contempt with financial or religious arguments: reading novels is a waste of valuable time, the only true book is the Bible, etc. I said that many Americans have been taught "to repress their imagination, to reject it as something childish or effeminate, unprofitable, and probably sinful. . . . They have learned to fear [the imagination]. But they have never learned to discipline it at all."

I wrote that in 1974. The millennium has come and we still fear dragons. Our fear has taken some forms I'd like to talk about.

One is the tactic of infantilizing fantasy. Fantasy is for children. It's kiddilit. It's cute. But fantasy also has shown that it can make money. Gotta take that seriously. So the Harry Potter books—amiable, conventional children's fantasies—were praised for their originality by reviewers utterly ignorant of the tradition they derive from: a tradition that descends from the *Mahabharata* and the *Ramayana*, the *One Thousand and One Nights* and *Beowulf* and the Tale of Monkey and medieval romance and Renaissance epic, through Kipling and Borges and Calvino and Rushdie: a form of literature that is not well described as cute, not to be dismissed as "entertainment," "great fun for the kiddies," or "well, at least they're reading *something."* The Potter phenomenon was a godsend to those who want fantasy to be childish, not to be taken seriously.

American critics and academics have been trying for forty years to bury one of the great works of twentieth-century fiction, *The Lord of the Rings.* They ignore it, they condescend to it, they stand in large groups with their backs to it, because they're afraid of it. They're afraid of dragons. They know if they acknowledge Tolkien they'll have to admit that fantasy can be literature, and that therefore they'll have to redefine what literature is.

What American critics and teachers call "literature" is still almost wholly restricted to realism. All other forms of fiction— westerns, mysteries, science fiction, fantasy, romance, historical, regional, you name it—are dismissed as "genre." Sent to the ghetto. That the ghetto is about twelve times larger than the city, and currently a great deal livelier, doesn't bother those who live in ivory towers. Magic realism, though—that does bother them; they hear Gabriel García Márquez gnawing quietly at the foundations of the ivory tower, they hear all these crazy Indians dancing up in the attic, and they think maybe they should do something about it. Perhaps they should give that fellow who teaches the science fiction course tenure? Oh, surely not.

To say that realistic fiction is by definition superior to imaginative fiction is to imply that imitation is superior to invention. I have wondered if this unstated but widely accepted (and, incidentally, very puritanical) proposition is related to the recent popularity of the memoir and the personal essay. This has been a genuine popularity, not a matter of academic canonizing. People really do want to read memoir and personal essay, and writers want to write it. I've felt rather out of step. I like history and biography fine, but when family and personal memoir seems to be the most popular—the dominant narrative form—well, I have searched my soul for prejudice and found it. I prefer invention to imitation. I love novels. I love made-up stuff.

To put a high value on story drawn directly from personal experience is a logical extension of our high value for realism in fiction. If fiction is expected to cling to actual experience, if faithful imitation of reality is its great virtue, then memoir is far more virtuous than fiction. The memoir writer's imagination is subordinated to the hard facts. It may connect them aesthetically and draw from them a moral or intellectual lesson but is understood to be forbidden to invent. If there's nothing in the story outside familiar experience, emotion may certainly be roused but imagination may scarcely be called upon. Recognition, rather than discovery, is the reward.

True recognition is a true reward. The personal essay is a noble and difficult discipline. I'm not knocking it. I admire it with considerable awe. But I'm not at home in it.

I keep looking for dragons in this country, and not finding any. Or only finding them in disguise.

Some of the most praised recent memoirs have been about growing up in hopeless poverty, cruel fathers, incompetent mothers, abused children, misery, fear, and loneliness. But is all this the property of nonfiction? Poverty, cruelty, incompetence, dysfunctional families, injustice, degradation—that is the very stuff of the fireside tale, the folk tale, stories of ghosts and vengeance beyond the grave—and of *Jane Eyre*, and *David Copperfield*, *Huckleberry Finn*, and *Cien años de soledad*. The ground of our experience is dark, and all our inventions start in that darkness. From it, some of them leap forth in fire.

The imagination can transfigure the dark matter of life. And in too many personal essays and autobiographies, that's what I begin to miss, to crave: transfiguration. To recognize our shared, familiar misery is not enough. I want to *recognize something I never saw before.* I want something terrible and blazing to leap out at me. I want the fire of the transfiguring imagination. I want the true dragons.

Experience is where ideas come from. But a story isn't a mirror of what happened. Fiction is experience translated by, transformed by, transfigured by the imagination. Truth includes but is not coextensive with fact. Truth in art is not imitation, but reincarnation.

To be valuable in a factual history, the raw material of experience has to be selected, arranged, and shaped. In a novel, the process is even more radical: the raw materials are not only selected and shaped but also fused, composted, recombined, reworked, reconfigured, reborn, and at the same time allowed to find their own forms and shapes, which may be only indirectly related to rational thinking—so that the whole thing may seem to be pure invention. A girl chained to a rock as a sacrifice to a monster. A mad captain and a white whale. A ring that confers absolute power. A dragon.

But there's no such thing as pure invention. Invention is recombination. We can work only with what we have. It all starts with experience. There are monsters and leviathans and chimeras in the human mind; they are psychic facts. Dragons are one of the truths about us. The only way we may be able to express that particular truth is by writing about dragons—admitting their existence. People who deny the existence of dragons are often eaten by dragons. From within.

Another way we show our distrust of the imagination, our puritanical lust to control it, is in the way we tell stories on TV and in video or online games.

Reading is active. To read a story is to participate actively in the story; to read is to tell the story to yourself by reliving it and rewriting it with the author, word by word, sentence by sentence, chapter by chapter. If you want proof, just watch an eight-year-old reading a story she likes. She is concentratedly, tensely, fiercely alive. She is as intense as a hunting cat.

Reading is a mysterious act. It absolutely has not and cannot be replaced by any kind of viewing, because viewing is an entirely different undertaking, with different stakes and rewards. Viewing is passive. A reader reading *makes* the book, brings it into meaning, by translating the arbitrary symbols, printed letters, into an inward, private reality. A viewer watching a film does not make the film. To watch a film is to be taken into it—to participate in it—be made part of it. Absorbed by it. Readers eat books, but film eats viewers. This is fine. It's wonderful to be eaten by a good movie, to let your eyes and ears take your mind into a reality you could never otherwise know. However, passivity means vulnerability, and that's what a great deal of media storytelling exploits.

Reading is an active transaction between the text and the reader. The text is under the control of the reader—she can skip, linger, interpret, misinterpret, return, ponder, go along with the story or refuse to go along with it, make judgments, revise her judgments—she has time and room to genuinely interact with it. A novel is an active, ongoing collaboration between the writer and the reader.

Viewing is not a transaction. It isn't collaborative. The viewer, consenting to participate, hands over control to the filmmaker or programmer. Psychically there is no time or room outside an audiovisual narrative for anything but the program. For the viewer, the monitor screen temporarily becomes the universe. There's very little leeway, and no way to control the constant stream of information and imagery unless one refuses to accept it and detaches oneself emotionally and intellectually, in which case it appears essentially meaningless. Or one can turn the program off.

Although there's a lot of talk about transactional viewing and "interactive" is a favorite word of programmers, electronic media are a paradise of control for programmers and a paradise of passivity for viewers. There is nothing in so-called interactive programs except what the programmer put in them; the so-called choices lead only to subprograms chosen by the programmer, no more a choice than a footnote is—do you read it or don't you. The roles in role-playing games are fixed and conventional; there are no characters, only personae. (That's why teenagers love them; teenagers need personae. But they have to shed those personae eventually, if they're going to become persons.) Hypertext offers the storyteller a wonderful complexity, but so far hypertext fiction seems to be like Borges's garden of forking paths that lead only to other forking paths—fascinating, like fractals, and ultimately nightmarish. Interactivity in the sense of the viewer controlling the text is also nightmarish, when interpreted to mean that the viewer can rewrite the novel. If you don't like the end of *Moby-Dick* you can change it. You can make it happy. Ahab kills the whale. Ooowee.

Readers can't kill the whale. They can only reread until they understand why Ahab made it kill him. Readers don't control the text: they genuinely interact with it. Viewers are either controlled by the program or try to control it. Different ballgames. Different universes.

A 3-D animated version of Saint-Exupéry's *The Little Prince*, narrated by Kenneth Branagh, appeared this year and was presented as offering "more than just the story of the Little Prince. You can, for example, catch an orbiting planet in the Little Prince's universe and learn all about the planet's secrets and its inhabitants." But in the book, doesn't the prince visit several planets, with extremely interesting inhabitants, and doesn't his own tiny planet have an immense secret—a rose—the rose he loves? Do the makers of this version feel that Saint-Exupéry was stingy with his planets? Or are they convinced that stuffing irrelevant information into a work of art enriches it? Maybe they'll give us a version of *The Tempest*, and when Miranda says, "O brave new world, that has such creatures in it!" the viewer can press a button and on the screen there will be information about a genuine virtual new world with all kinds of weird creatures in it.

We are told that the viewer can interact with the animated version of *The Little Prince*. You can "enter the Fox Training Game and after you've 'tamed' the fox that the Little Prince meets, he will give you a gift."

Do you remember the fox in *The Little Prince*? He insists that the little prince tame him. Why? the prince asks, and the fox says that if he is tamed he will always love the wheat fields, because they're the color of the little prince's hair. The little prince asks how to tame him, and the fox says by being very patient, sitting down "at a little distance from me . . . in the grass. I shall look at you out of the corner of my eye, and you will say nothing. Words are the source of misunderstandings. But you will sit a little closer to me, every day . . ." And it should be at the same time every day, so that the fox will "know at what hour my heart is to be ready to greet you . . . One must observe the proper rites." And so the fox is tamed, and when the little prince is about to leave, "'Ah,' said the fox, 'I shall cry.'" So the little prince laments that being tamed "has done you no good at all!" but the fox says, "It has done me good . . . because of the color of the wheat fields." And when they part, the fox says, "I will make you a present of a secret . . . It is the time you wasted for your rose that makes your rose important. . . . You become responsible, forever, for what you have tamed."

So, then, the child viewing the program "tames" the fox by pressing buttons until the food pellet drops into the food dish—no, no, sorry, that's how we train rats. We train children by teaching them to select the "right" choice from the choices offered until the program tells them that the fox is "tamed." Somehow this doesn't seem the same as imagining doing what the book describes: coming back every day at the same time and sitting silently while a fox looks at you out of the corner of its eye. Something essential has been short-circuited, falsified. What do you think the fox's "gift" to the child viewer will be? I don't know, but I don't really see how it can top the fox's gift in the book: just the words "you become responsible, forever, for what you have tamed."

The "gift" *The Little Prince* gives its readers is itself. It offers them absolutely nothing but a charming story with a few charming pictures, and the chance to face fear, grief, tenderness, and loss.

Which is why that story, written in the middle of a war by a man about to die in that war, is honored by children, adults, and even literary critics. Maybe the animated version isn't as ghastly as it sounds; but it's hard not to see it as an effort to exploit, to tame something that, like a real fox, must be left wild: the imagination of an artist.

Antoine de Saint-Exupéry did crash-land in the desert once, in the thirties, and nearly died; that is a fact. He did not meet a little prince from another planet there. He met terror, thirst, despair, and salvation. He wrote a splendid factual account of that experience in *Wind, Sand and Stars*. But later it got composted, transmuted, transfigured into a story of a little prince. Imagination working on experience. Invention springing like a flower, a rose, out of the desert sands of fact.

Thinking about the sources of art, about where ideas come from, we generally give experience too much credit. Biographers often seem not to realize that novelists make things up. They seek a direct source for everything in a writer's work, as if every character in a novel were based on a person the writer knew and every plot gambit had to mirror a specific actual event. Ignoring the incredible recombinatory faculty of the imagination, this fundamentalist attitude short-circuits the long, obscure process by which experience becomes story.

Where do you get your ideas? Oh, right here, right now, I just had this experience and I just met you and *bam*, and here's the story and you're in it! Yeah, sure.

Young writers earnestly tell me they'll start writing when they've gathered experience. Usually I keep my mouth shut, but sometimes I can't control myself and ask them, "Ah, like the Brontë sisters? Like Jane Austen?" Those women with their wild, mad lives crammed full of gut-wrenching adventure working as stevedores in the Congo, shooting up drugs in Rio, hunting lions on Kilimanjaro, having sex in Soho, and all that stuff that writers have to do—well, that some writers have to do.

Very young writers usually *are* handicapped by their relative poverty of experience. Even if their experiences are the stuff of which fiction can be made—and very often it's exactly the experiences of childhood and adolescence that feed the imagination for the rest of a writer's life—they don't have context, they don't yet have enough to compare it to. They haven't had time to learn that other people exist, people who have had similar experiences, and different experiences, and that they themselves will have different experiences, a breadth of comparison, a fund of empathic knowledge crucial to the novelist, who, after all, is making up a whole world.

So fiction writers are slow beginners. Very few are worth much till they're thirty or so. Not because they lack life experience, but because their imagination hasn't had time to compost it, to meditate on what they've done and seen and felt, and to realize its value may lie less in its uniqueness than in its giving access to an understanding of the shared human condition. This requires imaginative work, and autobiographical first novels, self-centered and self-pitying, often suffer from lack of imagination.

But many fantasies, works of so-called imaginative fiction, suffer from the same thing: imaginative poverty. The writers haven't actually used their imaginations, they don't make up anything— they just move archetypes around in a game of wish fulfillment.

In fantasy, since the fictionality of the fiction—the inventions, the dragons—are all right out in front, it's easy to assume that the story has no relation at all to experience, that everything in a fantasy can be just the way the writer wants. No rules, all cards wild. All the ideas in fantasy are just wishful thinking—right? Well, no. Wrong. It may be that the further a story gets away from common experience and accepted reality, the less wishful thinking it can do, and the more firmly its essential ideas must be grounded in common experience and accepted reality.

Serious fantasy goes into regions of the psyche that may be very strange territory to the reader, dangerous ground; and for that reason, serious fantasy is usually both conservative and realistic about human nature. Its mode is usually comic, not tragic; that is, it has a more-or-less happy ending but, just as the tragic hero brings his tragedy on himself, the happy outcome in fantasy is *earned* by the behavior of the protagonist. Serious fantasy invites the reader on a wild journey of invention, through wonders and marvels, through mortal risks and dangers—all the time hanging on to a common, everyday, realistic morality. Generosity, reliability, compassion, and courage: in fantasy these moral qualities are seldom questioned. They are accepted, and they are tested—often to the limit, and beyond.

The people who write the stuff on the book covers obsessively describe fantasy as "a battle between good and evil," but in commercial fantasy the battle is all it is; the white wizards and the black magicians are both mindlessly violent. It's not a moral struggle, just a power struggle. This is about as far from Tolkien as you can get.

But why should moral seriousness matter, why do probability and consistency matter, when it's "all just made up"? Well, moral seriousness is exactly what makes a fantasy matter. The made-up story is inevitably trivial if nothing real is at stake. That's my problem with Harry Potter; the powerful people are divided into good ones and bad ones, all of whom use their power for mere infighting and have nothing to do with people without power. Such easy wish fulfillment has a great appeal to children, who are genuinely powerless, but it worries me when adults fall for it. In the same way, the purer the invention, the more important is its credibility, consistency, and coherence. The rules of the invented realm must be followed to the letter. All wizards, including writers, are extremely careful about their spells. Every word must be the right word. A sloppy wizard is a dead wizard. Serious fantasists delight in invention, in the freedom to invent, but they know that careless invention kills magic. Fantasy happily flouts fact, but it is just as concerned with truth as the direst realism.

A related point: The job of the imagination, in making a story from experience, may be not to gussy the story up but to tone it down. The fact is, the world is unbelievably strange and human behavior is frequently so weird that no kind of narrative except farce or satire can handle it. The function of the storyteller's imagination sometimes is simply to make it more plausible.

The whole matter of "leaving it to the imagination" is enormously important. Even a journalist can't report the full event but can tell only bits of it, and the realist or fantasist leaves out a tremendous amount, *suggesting* through imagery or metaphors just enough that the reader can imagine the event. And the reader does just that. Story is a collaborative art. The writer's imagination works in league with the reader's imagination, calls on the reader to collaborate, fill in, flesh out, bring their own experience to the work. Fiction is not a camera and not a mirror. It's much more like a Chinese painting—a few lines, a few blobs, a whole lot of blank space, from which *we* make the travelers in the mist climbing the mountain toward the inn under the pines.

I want to use some of my own fiction as examples of Where Ideas Come From. I have written fantastic stories closely based on actual experience, and realistic stories totally made up out of whole cloth. Some of my science fiction is full of accurate and carefully researched fact, while my stories about ordinary people doing ordinary things on the Oregon coast in 1990 contain large wetlands and quicksands of pure invention. I hope to show you that fictional "ideas" arise from a combination of experience and imagination that is both indissoluble and utterly unpredictable.

In my Earthsea books, particularly the first one, people sail around on the sea in small boats all the time. They do it quite convincingly, and many people understandably assume that I spent years sailing around on the sea in small boats.

My entire experience with sailboats was during my junior semester at Berkeley High School, when they let us take sailing for gym credit. On a windy day in the Berkeley Marina, my friend Jean and I managed to overturn and sink a nine-foot catboat in three feet of water. We sang "Nearer, My God, to Thee" as she went down, and then waded a half mile back to the boathouse. The boatman was incredulous. "You *sank* it?" he said. "*How?*"

That will remain one of the secrets of the writer.

All right, so practically all the sailing in Earthsea, certainly all the deep-sea sailing, does not reflect experience. Not *my* experience. Only my imagination, using that catboat, other people's experience, novels I'd read, and some research (I do know why *Lookfar* is clinker-built), asking friends questions, and some trips on ocean liners. But basically, it's a fake. So is all the snow and ice in *The Left Hand of Darkness*. I never even saw snow till I was seventeen, and I certainly never pulled a sledge across a glacier. Except with Captain Scott, and Shackleton, and those guys. In books. Where do you get your ideas? From books, of course, from other people's books. If I didn't read, how could I write?

We all stand on each other's shoulders; we all use each other's ideas and skills and plots and secrets. Literature is a communal enterprise. That "anxiety of influence" stuff is just testosterone talking. Understand me: I don't mean plagiarism; I'm not talking about imitation, or copying, or theft. The stuff from other people's books gets into us just as our own experience does, is composted and transmuted and transformed by the imagination, just as actual experiences are, and comes forth entirely changed. If that were not so, if I thought I had really stolen and used any other writer's writing, I certainly wouldn't stand here congratulating myself. I'd go hide my head in shame and wait for the lawsuit. But as it is, I acknowledge with delight my endless debt to every storyteller I have ever read, my colleagues, my collaborators—I praise them and honor them, the endless givers of gifts.

So, in a science fiction novel set on a planet populated by people whose gender arrangements are highly imaginative, the part about two people hauling a sledge across a glacier is as factually accurate as

I could make it, down to the details of their gear and harness, how much weight they haul, how far they can get in a day, what different snow surfaces are like, and so on. None of this is from my direct experience; all of it is from the books I've read about the Antarctic, ever since I was in my twenties. It is factual material woven into a pure fantasy. As a matter of fact, so is all the stuff about their gender arrangements; but that's a little too complicated to go into here.

Once, I wanted to write a story from the point of view of a tree. The "idea" of the story came with the sight of an oak alongside the road to McMinnville, Oregon. I was thinking as we drove by that when the oak was young, Highway 18 was a quiet country road. I wondered what the oak thought about the highway, the cars. Well, so, where do I get the experience of being a tree, on which my imagination is to work? Books don't help much here. Unlike Shackleton and Scott, oaks don't keep diaries. Personal observation is my only experiential material. I have seen a lot of oaks, been around oaks, been in some oaks, externally, climbing around; now I want to be in one internally, inside. What does it feel like to be an oak? Large, for one thing; lively but quiet, and not very flexible except at the tips, out there in the sunlight. And deep—very deep—roots going down in the dark . . . To live rooted, to be two hundred years in *one* place, unmoving, yet traveling immensely through the seasons, the years, through time . . . Well, you know how it's done. You did it as a kid; you still do it. If you don't do it, your dreams do it for you. In dreams begins responsibility, said a poet. In dreams, in imagination, we begin to be one another. I am thou. The barriers go down.

A novel seldom comes from just one stimulus or "idea" but a whole clumping and concatenation of ideas and images, visions and mental perceptions, all slowly drawing in around some center that is usually obscure to me until long after the book's done and I finally say, "Oh, *that's* what that book's about." To me, two things are essential during this drawing together, the clumping process: before I know much of anything about the story I have to see the place, the landscape, and I have to know the principal people. By name. And it has to be the right name. If it's the wrong name, the character won't come to me. I won't know who the person is. The character won't talk, won't *do* anything. Please don't ask me how I arrive at the name and how I know it's the right name; I have no idea. When I hear it, I know it. And I know who the character is, and where. And then the story can begin.

Here is an example. My book *The Telling* started this way: I learned that Taoist religion, an ancient popular religion of vast complexity and a major element of Chinese culture, had been suppressed, wiped out, by Mao Tse-tung. Taoism as a practice now exists chiefly in Taiwan, possibly underground on the mainland, possibly not. In one generation, one psychopathic tyrant destroyed a tradition two thousand years old. In one lifetime. My lifetime. And I knew nothing about it. The enormity of the event, and the enormity of my ignorance, left me stunned. I had to think about it. Since the way I think is fiction, eventually I had to write a story about it. But how could I write a novel about China? My poverty of experience would be fatal. A novel set on an imagined world, then, about the extinction of a religion as a deliberate political act in counterpoint to the suppression of political freedom by a theocracy? All right, there's my theme, my idea if you will.

I'm impatient to get started, impassioned by the theme. So I look for the people who will tell me the story, the people who are going to live this story. And I find this uppity kid, this smart girl who goes from Earth to that world. I don't remember what her original name was; she had five different names. I started the book five times, and it got nowhere. I had to stop.

I had to sit, patiently, and say nothing, at the same time every day, while the fox looked at me out of the corner of its eye and slowly let me get a little bit closer. And finally the woman whose story it was spoke to me. "I'm Sutty," she said. "Follow me." So I followed her; and she led me up into the high mountains; she gave me the book.

I had a good idea; but I did not have a story. The story had to make itself, find its center, find its voice—Sutty's voice. Then, because I was waiting for it, it could give itself to me. Or put it this way: I had a lot of stuff in my head, but I couldn't pull it together, I couldn't dance that dance because I hadn't waited to catch the beat. I didn't have the rhythm.

Earlier, I used a sentence from a letter from Virginia Woolf to her friend Vita Sackville-West. Sackville-West had been pontificating about finding the right word, Flaubert's *mot juste*, and agonizing very Frenchly about style; and Woolf wrote back, very Englishly:

> As for the *mot juste*, you are quite wrong. Style is a very simple matter; it is all rhythm. Once you get that, you can't use the wrong words. But on the other hand here am I sitting after half the morning, crammed with ideas, and visions, and so on, and can't dislodge them, for lack of the right rhythm. Now this is very profound, what rhythm is, and goes far deeper than words. A sight, an emotion, creates this wave in the mind, long before it makes words to fit it; and in writing (such is my present belief) one has to recapture this, and set this working (which has nothing apparently to do with words) and then, as it breaks and tumbles in the mind, it makes words to fit it: But no doubt I shall think differently next year.

Woolf wrote that seventy-five years ago; if she did think differently next year, she didn't tell anybody. She says it lightly, but she means it: this is very profound. I have not found anything more profound, or more useful, about the source of story—where the ideas come from.

Beneath memory and experience, beneath imagination and invention—beneath *words*, as she says—there are rhythms to which memory and imagination and words all move. The writer's job is to go down deep enough to begin to feel that rhythm, find it, move to it, be moved by it, and let it move memory and imagination to find words.

She's full of ideas but she can't dislodge them, she says, because she can't find their rhythm—can't find the beat that will unlock them, set them moving forward into a story, get them telling themselves. A "wave in the mind," she calls it; and says that a sight or an emotion may create it, like a stone dropped into still water, and the circles go out from the center in silence, in perfect rhythm, and the mind follows those circles outward and outward till they turn to words. But her image is greater: her wave is a sea wave, traveling smooth and silent a thousand miles across the ocean till it strikes the shore and crashes, breaks, and flies up in a foam of words. But the wave, the rhythmic impulse, is before words and "has nothing to do with words." So the writer's job is to recognize the wave, the silent swell way out at sea, way out in the ocean of the mind, and follow it to shore, where it can turn or be turned into words, unload its story, throw out its imagery, pour out its secrets. And ebb back into the ocean of story.

What is it that prevents the ideas and visions from finding their necessary underlying rhythm, why couldn't Woolf "dislodge" them that morning? It could be a thousand things, distractions, worries; but very often I think what keeps a writer from finding the words is that she grasps at them too soon, hurries, grabs. She doesn't wait for the wave to come in and break. She wants to write because she's a writer; she wants to say this, and tell people that, and show people something else—things she knows, her ideas, her opinions, her beliefs, important things—but she doesn't wait for the wave to come and carry her beyond all the ideas and opinions, to where you *cannot use the wrong word*. None of us is Virginia Woolf, but I hope every writer has had at least a moment when they rode the wave, and all the words were right.

Prose and poetry—all art, music, dance—rise from and move with the profound rhythms of our body, our being, and the body and being of the world. Physicists read the universe as a great range of vibrations, of rhythms. Art follows and expresses those rhythms. Once we get the beat, the right beat, our ideas and our words dance to it—the round dance that everybody can join. And then I am thou, and the barriers are down. For a while.

On "Beauty"

MARILYNNE ROBINSON

January 19, 2006

It has seemed to me for some time that beauty, as a conscious element of experience, as a thing to be valued and explored, has gone into abeyance among us. I do not by any means wish to suggest that we suffer from any shortage of beauty, which seems to me intrinsic to experience, everywhere to be found. The pitch of a voice, the gesture of a hand, can be very beautiful. I need hardly speak of daylight, warmth, silence. When I was a girl too young to give the matter any thought at all, I used to be overcome by the need to write poetry whenever there was a good storm, that is, heavy rain and wind enough to make the house smell like the woods. I wrote in a style both tragic and passé. If I had known the word, I would have probably titled all my poems "Threnody." They were inevitably lamed by my inability to think of enough good rhymes. I knew there were things amiss with them, and I hid them under my mattress and never looked at them again. I cannot claim to have been the Emmeline Grangerford of northern Idaho, because there were other serious contenders for that title in my personal acquaintance. No matter. I felt, when the fit was upon me, the purest desire to interpret into language whatever it was I felt in the storm. Nothing remarkable in that, but for me the experience was important if only because I've never really outgrown it. The old passion is gone, and the poetry, and I am no longer quite so exclusively under the spell of Edgar Allan Poe, God rest his soul. But that old sense that I must try to be an interpreter of the true and absolute world, the very planet, that has remained. I once attempted a rather melancholy poem about Being Itself, but was stymied once again by the insufficiency of rhymes.

I was supported in all this by a lingering romanticism, by Wordsworth and Keats at school, and, at my grandparents' house, by a far too lovely painting of the moon. Remarkable as it seems to me in retrospect, the only students in my high school who were given the skills they would need to be employable were the ones who were not considered to be up to much else. My own education was sublimely impractical, and therefore it encouraged me, always implicitly, to feel that my way of thinking about things had value. Not that anyone encouraged aspiration in me; not that I aspired; it was all much purer than that. I had, in a stuffy and provincial form, cultural permission to be attracted to what seemed to me to be beautiful. I memorized so much poetry, most of it dreadful, of course, and no one ever asked me why. They would have known why—because most of it seemed beautiful to me. I went to college and was instructed in more rigorous standards, and I am very grateful for that, needless to say.

The word *beauty* has always seemed to me unsatisfactory. I have often felt there is an essential quality for which we have no word, and that therefore I am driven back on *beauty*, or *elegance*, which has the same problem. It is interesting that both these words are French, that they displaced Old English precursors. In any case, the word *beauty* has never seemed to me quite suited to the uses I have had to make of it, as though it were never really naturalized into my interior language, or what I might call my aesthetic experience, if that did not oblige me to use the word *aesthetic*. Why this awkwardness? Why must we lapse into French or Greek to speak of an experience that is surely primary and universal? Perhaps the awkwardness of the language refers to the fact that the experience of beauty is itself complex. We all know we can be conditioned to see beauty where our culture or our generation tells us to see it. Not so very long ago, fashionable American women carried little vials of arsenic along with their powder and hairpins, a dose that gave them a pallor that was considered lovely at the time, though to an objective eye it must have resembled death. And we know beauty can be fraudulent, compromised. Whenever power or privilege wishes to flaunt itself, it recruits beauty into its service, or something that can at least pass as beauty and will achieve the same effect. So it is entirely appropriate to regard beauty with a critical eye. But the point should be to discover an essential beauty, not to abandon the intuition altogether.

American literature, back in the days when we still remembered the Revolution, aspired to an aesthetic of simplicity, of common speech, and of common circumstance. These things seen under the aspect of very grand thought, of course. Eternity is as far as to the very nearest room. Then plain speech in our literature became the sign of plain thought, mental and spiritual entrapment, and, after that, this grievous state of soul came to be seen as all that plain language could possibly render. This lowered evaluation seems to have become entrenched about the time of the Depression, and to have become the condescension that mistakes itself for fellow feeling. I generalize too broadly. Faulkner is one great exception, and there are others. But American realism and naturalism seem to me to have broken speech into two dialects: an authentic speech that addresses simple thought and immediate experience, often victimized or degraded experience, and an artificial and essentially suspect speech for those who express ideas. We have educated a larger proportion of our population than any civilization in history, yet a candidate for president can be pilloried for letting slip a word the press considers vaguely recondite. The prejudice against learned language reinforces the notion that those who speak ordinary American English can't have much on their minds. More recently, the flood of French into universities has certainly compounded the problem, since it encourages the use of a jargon that would be laughable in a novel, or on the editorial page, or in conversation with a friend. In any case, we do not now have a dialect that allows us to speak naturally about ideas, at least in fiction. Whether this is less true for other areas of discourse I cannot say, since the attempt seems to be made so rarely.

The nineteenth century was right. Ordinary language can do as much as the mind can ask of it, and do it with extraordinary integrity. What we have lost with this awareness is respect for people in general, to whom we condescend, as though we were not all ourselves members in good standing of people in general. We explain others to ourselves without reference to what were once called their souls, to their solitary and singular participation in this mystery of being. We are not much in awe of one another these days. We do not hesitate to deprive each other of dignity or privacy, or even to deprive ourselves of them. In saying this, I am speaking of the media, journalism, and publishing, which, for all anyone knows, are no true gauge of what public feeling is, or what it could be if it formed under other influences or had other choices. The problem I am describing is not local and it is certainly not new. The emergence of democracy awaited the rise of respect for people in general, and it will not outlive its decline. What reason can there be for protecting the privacy and freedom of the conscience, or even the franchise, of anyone, if we assume nothing good about those whom we are protecting and enfranchising? There is much talk about the polarization of this country. Most disturbing, I think, is the way both sides are of one mind, and they are of one mind in this: neither acts in a way that acknowledges the beauty and complexity of individual human experience. Neither treats the public—the people—with real respect. Lately, there has been talk to the effect that science has lowered humankind in its own estimation. This notion has a very long history going back to the time when grave damage was thought to have been done by the discovery that the earth was no longer the center of the universe.

There are those who believe we have outlived every beautiful notion about what human life must be, because this is the age of science. These people must not have been paying attention. Science, being one of the unequivocally human undertakings, describes humanity to itself, for weal and woe, in everything it does. Mathematicians and physicists have a habit of using the words *beautiful* and *elegant* to endorse theories that are likelier to cleave to the nature of things because of their efficiency and soundness of structure. I would like to see language brought to a similar standard. If this were at all a philosophic age, we might be wondering why it is that beauty can test reality and solve its encryptions in the modest, yet impressive, degree our humanity allows. For me, this is a core definition of beauty: that it is both rigorous and dynamic and that it somehow bears a deep relationship to truth. If I seem to be brushing up against logical positivism, I assure you that in taking statements that science produces as norms of proof, I mean only that we are part of a mystery, a splendid mystery within which we must attempt to orient ourselves if we are to have a sense of our own nature. I say this knowing that contemporary science suggests—with its talk of unexpressed dimensions of reality and the effect of the observer on what seems to us to be autonomous and objective reality—that the apparent lawfulness of nature can seem to be what the old philosopher Jonathan Edwards said it was: a courtesy to our limitations. I believe that there is a penumbra of ignorance and error and speculation that exceeds what might be called the known world by a very large factor indeed. I believe this penumbra is as beautiful in its own way as what I have called truth because it is the action of the human consciousness. It is most human and most beautiful because it wants to be more than consciousness; it wants to be truth.

Admiring the cosmos carries certain risks in these contentious times. It sounds like piety. It sounds, more specifically, like an argument for intelligent design. Oddly, great areas of science are closed off from consideration by people who take themselves to be defenders of science, precisely because it is impossible not to marvel at the things science reveals. Controversy has not gone well in this country for some time, and there could be no better illustration of that fact than that, at this moment, when gorgeous hypotheses bloom day after day, when the heavens should be as wonderful to us as to the Babylonians, we refuse to look up from a quarrel we've carried on now for 150 years. Anyone who reads an occasional article on genetic research knows that both change and stability are more mysterious than the simple mechanisms of Darwin, championed by writers such as Richard Dawkins, can by any means acknowledge. On the other hand, anyone who has read a little good theology, or encountered a devout mind, is perfectly aware that religion does not hang on the question of the origin of species. I have read that there are great spiral structures in space so vast that no account can be made of them, no hypothesis made to describe their formation, and they appear somehow to have their own weather, so to speak. To what can we compare these things but to the mind that discovered and described them, the human mind, which, over the centuries, has amassed by small increments the capacity for knowing about them. Planet earth is not even a speck of dust in the universe, and how uncanny it is that we have contrived to see almost to the edge of what time and light will allow, to look back billions of years and see suns forming. When I read about such things, I think how my own heroes would have loved them. What would Melville have done with dark energy, or Poe with spooky action at a distance? Whitman could only have loved the accelerating expansion of the universe. Dickinson probably knew already that our sun is atremble with sound waves, like a great gong. It is a loss of the joy of consciousness that keeps us from appropriating these splendors for the purposes of our own thought.

Religion, or at least those religions that derive from poor, battle-weary Genesis, has believed that humankind holds a privileged and central place in the created order. I am very far from suggesting that by this privilege was meant so trivial a thing as the capacity of knowing on a scale almost commensurate for grandeur with the universe in which we are so trivial a presence. I'm no believer in proofs. John Ames and I are very much of one mind on that point. But perhaps we should note in the insights of the ancients another thing at which to marvel. They recognized a special destiny for humankind, when grueling labor and early death would have consumed most of them. The destiny we have made for ourselves may well be the end of us; we all know that, and they seem to have known it too. Still, there is magnificence in it all. So the supposed conflict of science and religion is meaningless, because these two most beautiful ventures of expression of the human spirit are reduced to disembodied fragments of themselves with no beauty about them at all, which is a great pity, since their beauty should have been the basis for harmony between them.

When I wrote *Gilead*, I used the plain voice suited to the place and character. I've been very gratified by the responsive readers who found the language moving and at the same time noticed how ordinary it really is. Plain language has a strong, subtle music in it, which is intimately related to its capacity for meaning. I think every significant American poet before the modern period set out to prove this point. The fad for too long now has been to try to find the hermeneutics of practically everything, to find the agenda behind what is said, which in general seems to mean a scheme to enhance the interests of one's demographic. One hears the phrase "a hermeneutics of suspicion." All this brings to a text a reading that exists apart from the text, so whatever a writer might attempt or intend can be dismissed as self-distraction or camouflage. Then why listen for a distinctive music in the language? Why watch for a characterizing gesture? I have read that literacy has fallen among college graduates, that they are less capable of taking in the explicit sense of an editorial, for example. I suspect they were only practicing their hermeneutics: deconstructing, prying out an agenda, since attending to an explicit meaning would be like tossing the coffee and eating the paper cup. Quite simply, to approach any utterance as if its meaning were separable from its presentation is to disallow art in every positive sense of that word. It is to strip away the individuation that might make a work a new witness, and it is to violate the bond of reader and writer. The essence of our art lies in creating a lingering dream, good or bad, that other souls can enter. Dreaming one's soul into another's is an urgent business of the human mind: the dreaming itself, not whatever agenda can supposedly be extracted from it. As art, it plays on the nerves and the senses like a dream. It unfolds over time like a dream. It makes its own often disturbing and often inexplicable appeal to memory and emotion, creating itself again in the consciousness of the reader or hearer. There have always been people for whom all this makes no sense, but the refusal to take literature on its own terms somehow came to seem sophisticated and swept the universities. Stranger things have happened, I suppose.

In any case, fiction has the character of a hypothesis, or it is written in an implied subjunctive, because it means that reality is greater than any present circumstance. It says, "I will show you how that past or other or potential reality might feel, how it might look." And here I wish to say again that the beauty of language is rigorous and exploratory: it creates consent to, and participation in, a sense of coherency that is something like the fabric of experience itself. Anyone who makes the effort can find four or five scientific cosmologies, all of them substantially wrong, no doubt, and all perhaps in some part right. They are webs of possibility fashioned from conjecture and observation, and every one of them is human consciousness projected on that starry void from which humankind has never been able to turn its gaze. How strange it is that no new thought comes from these new heavens. Copernicus and Galileo moved the world, so to speak, with ideas that were fundamentally far less astonishing than those that have come in the last few decades. The effect of this abeyance of beauty of which I have been speaking is very general in contemporary experience. Everything we are asked to look at is abrupt, bright, and loud in the visual sense of the word, especially the evening news. We are expected to react to it, not to consider it. It is addressed to our nervous systems, never to our minds. I know the assumptions at work here, and none of them is a compliment to the public or, to employ older language, to the people. There is no inevitability in any of it. The visual technologies are blamed, but in fact no more beautiful studies of the human face exist than those made in film while it was still possible for the camera to pause for a moment.

I spoke before about the epic battle between parody science and parody religion. Anything stripped of the beauty and dignity proper to it is a parody. Public life itself is now entirely too vivid an instance of this phenomenon. We are losing an atmosphere that is necessary to our survival. We are losing the motive and the rationale that supported everything we claim to value. But the solution is everywhere around us and is as simple as seeing and hearing. We are a grand and tragic creature, humankind, and we must see ourselves as we are—quite possibly the greatest wonder of creation, alone in our capacity for awe, and in that fact altogether worthy of awe. We know that humankind has sat around its fires from time immemorial and told its tales and told them again, elaborating and refining, and we know that certain of these tales have become myth, epic, fable, Holy Writ. Now, because we have devoted so much ingenuity to the project, we have devised more ways to tell ourselves more stories, which means only that an ancient impulse is still so strong in us as to impel the invention of new means and occasions for telling and hearing to satisfy this appetite for narrative. At the most fundamental level, narrative is how we make sense of things—that is, our experience of ongoing life is a story we tell ourselves, more or less true, depending on circumstance. I believe this narrative is the essential mode of our being in the world, individually and collectively. Maintaining its integrity— maintaining a sense of the essentially provisional or hypothetical character of the story we tell ourselves—is, I will suggest, our greatest practical, as well as moral and ethical, problem. Fiction is narrative freed from the standard of literal truth. In effect, it is the mind exploring itself, its impulse to create hypothetical cause and consequence.

I know there is nothing fashionable about putting active consciousness at the center of a discussion of what we are. I know phrases like "our being in the world" are considered extremely suspect, if they are considered at all. If my language is somewhat romantic, it is so in reaction against an inappropriate reductionism that especially afflicts the discussion of consciousness, and which cannot at all address the experience of reading, hearing, or creating narrative. Nor can it, for that matter, address thought. There is, of course, the honorable strategy of inquiry called reductionism, which narrows a question in order to clarify it, and there is a very bad habit, also called reductionism, which is a tendency to forget that the question has been narrowed, and narrowed provisionally, in service to the understanding of the complexity in which it is in fact embedded.

Yes, we share consciousness with cats and dogs. They can interpret the sound of the refrigerator door opening, and we can interpret a ballad or a mathematical formula. However, with all respect to animals, there are real limits to the usefulness of the analogy they provide. Our extraordinary complexity is not only our distinction among the animals and our glory but also our tragedy, our capacity to do extraordinary harm. We may have most of our genome in common with the higher primates, as well as with pigs and fungi, it seems, but we are the only creatures who would ever have thought to split the atom. This is an instance of our unique ability to get ourselves into the worst kind of trouble, to create trouble this seismic world, left to itself, would have spared us. To err is human; to err catastrophically is definitively human. Our capacity for error at its most beautiful can be seen as the ability to make tentative models of reality and then reject them. We are certainly unique in our drive to know very much more than we need to know, and this capacity for making and rejecting has been crucial through the unfathomable amount of learning we have done since it first occurred to us to fashion a primitive weapon. Reductionism that would make us unique chiefly for our upright stance and our opposable thumbs sounds tough-minded. But I suspect its great appeal lies in its exclusion of the data to be drawn from our unique history as the makers and products of civilization. The neo-Darwinists insist that we, and our behavior, are formed around the project of ensuring our genetic survival. History should be a sufficient rebuttal.

I tend to draw analogies from science because I believe that our sense of the world is always hypothesis, and we are sane in the sense that we understand this. To proceed by hypothesis is the method of modern science, ideally. It is one of the dominant assumptions of modern culture that science, by its nature, drives back the shadows of error. It is this confidence that very often leads science to forget skepticism and to take itself for the unique domain of truth. Many of the darkest shadows of the modern period have been the products of science, and there is no reason to call it by any other name than science simply because it was grossly in error. Racial theory and eugenics are cases in point. I say this because I wish to assert that all thought always inclines toward error. The prejudices that would exclude one tradition of thought, be it science or be it theology, from this tendency are simply instances of the tendency toward error.

Narrative is the strategy of the mind for putting things in relation. I know I assume many things by using such a term as "the mind," or by suggesting that it could by its nature have such a thing as a strategy. I believe I am proceeding at least by analogy with things science tells us: for example, that heart cells beat, and that brain cells seem to be independently capable of cognition. I have never read an account of the processes by which healing occurs in the body or pathogens are dealt with by the immune system that did not invite the use of the word *tactic* or *strategy*. The ability to put things in relation—to say, "If this, then that," or even, "And then and then"—is as essential to our survival as the ability to heal. Therefore, in speaking of the mind, I think it is reasonable to assume an intrinsic purpose of complexity of the kind that one finds in every other physical system. Of course, failure is the snake in the Garden in every one of these systems, brilliant as they are. Just so, the mind is prolific in generating false narrative. Like the immune system, it can turn against itself, defeat itself.

It has lately been fashionable to say, quoting Nietzsche, that there is no fact, only interpretation. This itself is an interpretation of the fact that in our efforts to understand the world, we ordinarily get things a little wrong—sometimes very wrong. Fact does break through interpretation when it startles us, shames us, or kills us. I would say that every utterance, except the very slightest one, feels the pull of error, a sort of impalpable and irresistible gravity exerted on it by habit, assumption, fear, by the mass of presumed knowledge that is itself shaped by the same pull of error. I would say also that this bias away from truth is reinforced by the character of language itself. Language makes sense without reference to the truth, or with an oblique or even an inverted reference to it. So why have we sat around our fires these last dozen millennia, telling each other stories? What are we doing when we write fiction? What is the value of intentional untruth, acknowledged as such by teller and hearer, writer and reader? Granting that, at its best, fiction can be said to express a "higher truth"—I will not for the moment attempt a definition of that phrase—the great majority of the tales we tell have more modest aspirations, or they rehearse and reinforce conventional notions, or play on prejudice or fear. If, as I have said, narratives are always false in some degree, then perhaps fiction might be called the creative exploration of the tendency of narrative toward falsification, or toward the inevitable primacy of mind and language over objective fact in any account we attempt to make of the unfolding of the phenomenal world. Fiction might also be called the creative exploration of the power of narrative to enlist belief, even in the absence of what we ordinarily call credibility. Or, if we are at ease in the world of fabrication, perhaps this is so because every construction we make of the world is, or should be, hypothetical. It is a story we tell ourselves. Being hypothetical, it is also at best falsifiable. We believe we understand someone; we find we've been wrong when we hurt them or they hurt us. We think we know how we are perceived and valued, and learn that those around us have quite another view of us, far better or far worse. I might suggest that we are sane in the degree that our internal narrative retains the character of hypothesis, permitting editing, necessary adjustment, the assimilation of new understanding. Fictional narratives consistently employ surprise, reversal, irony, hidden identity. The wandering Ulysses is continually confronted with prodigies that alter the effective terms of survival. Only his shrewdness, his ability to respond to urgencies that constantly change, allows him to return alive to Ithaca. Disrupted hypothesis is structured into fiction of all kinds, from *Don Quixote* to "Casey at the Bat." Freud used Sophocles to illustrate his thesis, and so will I. Oedipus the king understands himself as wise, virtuous, and fortunate. In the course of the tragedy, he learns that in every way he has considered himself to have been fortunate, virtuous, and wise, he has in fact lived out a destiny that can only lead him to misery and exile, to something worse than disgrace. He was doomed to misunderstand, to live by an utterly false hypothesis, so perfect in its seeming consistency with experience that it was destroyed all at once, suddenly, catastrophically. For the rest of us, at best we remind ourselves that there are always limits to what we can know, that things are not always as they appear to us. These fictions I have described are in fact multiple narratives, the one that has the initial appearance of truth, the truer narrative that disrupts it, and then the overarching narrative that tells us that the best of us and the wisest of us can sometimes be very wrong. At our worst, we fall into inappropriate certainty. In individuals, this can be anything from irksome to pathological. In societies, it can be literally atrocious.

Perhaps one function of fiction is to train us in the fact of the intrinsic plausibility of narrative, that is, to practice us in acknowledging the fact that plausibility is no guarantee of truth, that plausibility can be merely an effect of intelligibility, compounded by fantasy, or fear, or worse. Elvis is alive and bussing tables in a truck stop in Arizona. Extraterrestrials take an uncivil interest in the anatomy of earthlings. Jesus eloped with Mary Magdalene to the South of France. These narratives flourish as they do under a thin pretense of journalism and a thinner pretense of scholarship. Clearly, acknowledged fiction does not teach us the lesson well enough, that we are inescapably error prone, and that what strikes us as plausible has no necessary relation to truth. We need only consider the potency of the blood libel against the Jews or the impact of the Protocols of the Elders of Zion or, more recently, the British document that seemed to confirm the suspicion that Saddam Hussein possessed weapons of mass destruction.

I have a theory about this moment in American history. We have all forgotten what ought to be the hypothetical character of our thinking. I know I have described the ability to absorb and

135

modify as the mark of sanity, and I wish only to underscore this view. The problem at the most obvious level is the much-noted disappearance of the art of compromise. In general, we are inappropriately loyal to our hypotheses, rather than to the reality of which they are always a tentative sketch. This is a special problem in a climate of urgency and anxiety. In the privacy of the classroom, as aware as they are of the afflicted state of the world, my students sometimes ask me if I have any explanation for what we are doing there. Why write fiction, they ask, and why read it? What does it mean, why does it matter? They are themselves engrossed in the art as writers and readers, and yet they ask these questions, and I have had to give a great deal of thought to their questions in order to feel that I can reply in a way that can do them any kind of justice. It might never have occurred to me to answer these questions if my students had not expected me to know the answers. I tell them we are doing something so ancient, so pervasive, and so central to human culture that we can assume its significance, even if we cannot readily describe or account for it. There is no reason to suppose the invention of narrative is in any way a marginal activity. Narratives define whole civilizations to themselves, for weal or woe. It surprises my students a little to find themselves placed in continuity with humankind, since they have been encouraged to believe, as I have also been encouraged to believe, that, as moderns, we are on the far side of a rupture in the history of civilization that makes all that we do different in kind from all that went before. I am telling them that they should follow the grain of their humanity, that words are beautiful and thoughts are shapely, and that they participate in the mystery of these facts as surely as Shakespeare ever did. They have been taught, as I was taught also, that the modern experience has brought with it certain disillusionments, typically unspecified though sometimes invoking the First

World War, that sometimes curtail aspiration or even embarrass it. The wisdom we have supposedly acquired in the course of our disillusionment has given us to know that the great questions are closed, and they are closed not because they have been answered but because we now know they were meaningless to begin with, no matter how handsomely they may have figured in *The Epic of Gilgamesh* or *Paradise Lost*. Fond as I am of the old great ideas and persuaded as I am that they did not die from the excesses of the twentieth or nineteenth or seventeenth centuries, and that they did not perish under the razor of logical positivism, I really do not believe that they are the only great ideas of which the species is capable. It is because we have isolated them as illusions and imagined ourselves to be beyond illusions that, in putting them aside, we have—by no means inevitably—foreclosed the possibility of new grand thought. There has been a pronounced tendency for the last four centuries or so to demystify the mind and the self. It was a project of early modern science, and it is a tendency still vigorously present, not much changed by the passage of time and the advance of neuroscience. Not coincidentally, it is very much in harmony with the neo-utilitarianism of our cultural moment, as well as with the fads of illness and cure or of dysfunction and reformation that seem always to entrance our public, caught forever, as they always seem to be, between anxiety or self-disparagement and undashable hope.

There is an economic rationale at work here, favoring a demystified view. If the operations of the mind are assumed by the public to be simple and standard, these fads can of course be mass-marketed. And there is the belief that Americans in particular are in fact a bit stupid, that their emotions are few and primitive. It is this belief that led to our own recent oddly Maoist cultural revolution, the intentional dumbing down of everything in our collective life that requires or reflects intelligence and even minimal education, except, perhaps, for tax forms and the fine print on the backs of credit card applications. Stupid is not a dialect that can tell us anything we need to know, and we have installed it as the language of journalism and public life to truly regrettable effect. Who would deny this? Yet the prejudice that insists on finding an essential simplicity in the human brain, sometimes called the most complex object known to exist in the universe, retains its authority.

The human situation is beautiful and strange. We are in fact Gilgamesh and Oedipus and Lear. We have achieved this amazing levitation out of animal circumstance by climbing our rope of sand, insight, and error—corrective insight and persistent error. The working of the mind is astonishing and beautiful. I remember two lines from a poem I learned in high school: "Let not young souls be smothered out before / they do strange deeds and fully flaunt their pride." That poem protested poverty, as I recall, but privilege can smother too, and the best education can smother if the burden of it is to tell the young that they need not bother being young, to distract them from discovering the pleasures of their own brilliance, and to persuade them that basic humanity is an experience closed to them.

My theory of narrative as a fundamental act of consciousness implies to me that paranoia might be entrapment in a bad narrative, and depression may be the inability to sustain narrative. I believe we are collectively putting ourselves at risk of both paranoia and depression. In an earlier paragraph, I put the question of the higher meaning that can sometimes be achieved in fiction. I would say that meaning is essentially a new discovery of the joy of consciousness—and, of course, the perils of it. We live in uncertainty, which means that we are always exposed to the possibility of learning more, for weal and woe. I would call this awareness humanism, an ultimate loyalty to ourselves that we are all too ready to withhold.

Fiction to Make Sense of Life

WALLACE STEGNER

November 20, 1990

When I was young and trying to learn to write—I used to study the manuals, you know, they used to have all these manuals, how to do this and how to write, hoping that there was a way, and that it could be learned—I remember once going to a lecture entitled "How to Write a Short Story Though Ignorant." Knowing my own ignorance, though not especially humble about it, even then, I thought that a humorous man who started from right where I was might be able to teach me something. That was a vain hope. The ignorance in the man's title was a come-on. He knew *exactly* how to write a short story. He had a bottle into which he could pour any mixture, and over the years he'd confirmed his confidence in the method by selling the product of his bottling works to the *Saturday Evening Post* for high prices. For him, a story was made, not born or discovered or achieved. And if it began as something discovered in life, it was not a story until it had been tugged and pulled into a pattern—to fit a pattern. Every story for him began with a carefully constructed situation with the seeds of conflict in it. Two men were rivals for a girl or a gold mine or a corporation. They were evenly matched, and only the most tenuous and sometimes deceptive clues told the reader which was the good guy and which was the bad guy. They didn't seem that much different. First one held the advantage, then the other. Seesaw game. But a smart writer dropped hints suggesting that the one who was really going to lose looked more like the winner—just for suspense. And at the point of greatest complication, it should seem that the bad guy, who was by now beginning to be suspected and disliked, would win. And then as swiftly and economically and plausibly as possible, something was introduced or revealed that turned things around. The bad guy went under; the good guy came out on top, as in "Cinderella" and many other basic plots that could be looked up in Polti's *Thirty-Six Dramatic Situations*. By the time the denouement was reached, a reader would realize that he had been hoping, all the time, for this solution that now seemed inevitable.

Since I sought instruction from that ignorant lecturer, I've written a few dozen short stories and a dozen or more novels, and I'm willing to grant that his method of the plotted story, of the complication resolved, which is as old as storytelling itself and about as much in fashion as Oxford bags, can still be effective and artful in the right hands and the right circumstances, and when informed with real passion. Conflict still is the essence of drama, no matter how we attenuate it or etherealize it or cover it up. Winning and losing are still endings that people care about. And last-minute winnings and endings are the most dramatic and satisfying of all, as when, a week or so ago, Stanford scored nine points in the last twelve seconds of play.

The ordinary patterning of a story in the old-fashioned way used to be reversal of expectation—lead a reader to think that something is going to happen and turn it on its head and surprise him a little. The movies and the TV prove that every day. And even stories that seem to avoid entirely the calculation and the manipulation implicit in reversals can be seen, when you look at all closely, still to be reversals. Look at John Cheever's story "Torch Song," in which you are shown a young girl from the Middle West who comes to New York. She looks like everybody's friend and companion; she helps people out; she's always sitting by bedsides. You go through her whole career until he turns the last page and shows you necrophilia. She's in love with death; she's in love with sickness. That's a reversal of what you have thought of her all along, and yet when you know it, it's the way the story has to go. Or take another Cheever, "The Swimmer," which looks like the story of a well-to-do suburbanite going home through swimming pools and cocktail parties to his well-cared-for house. And at the last page he meets a locked door; he's closed out, his career has ended, he has just been walking toward, essentially, his death, through the whole story. Or take one like William Faulkner's "A Rose for Emily," where we're told a story of about twenty years of old Emily, who's lived in a shut-up house behind drawn blinds—there have been episodes when strange odors emanated—and the neighbors went around surreptitiously throwing lime at the foundations, thinking some skunk had got under the house and died or something. It turns out that Emily, who was engaged to a Yankee contractor after the Civil War, was abandoned, ditched by this man who disappeared, and that's when she disappeared into her house behind the drawn blinds. When she dies, they enter her house finally— you know this story, undoubtedly—and find, in her bedroom, the corpse of the contractor, melted into the bed. It's been there ever since she closed up the house. And in the pillow beside it, the dent of another head. So Emily has not only murdered her faithless lover but has slept with his corpse. You think, "Well, all right, that's a pretty good Faulkner touch." But then you look more closely, and in the last line you see in that dent, in the pillow beside the corpse, an iron-gray hair. She's not only slept with his corpse, but she's been sleeping with it ever since, for twenty years. And that's an extra little touch, you know, an extra kicker to reverse your expectations a little bit and also to add an incomparably Faulknerian-gothic detail and give you some notion of a kind of intransigent Southern pride, which is really what the theme of that story is.

Listening to that lecturer long ago, I didn't grant any validity to all of his traditional formulas and reversals. I was offended that he tried to sell me that old routine carpentry of storytelling. Though I might have granted that conflict was still the essence of drama, I disliked the contrivance and manipulation that conflict seemed to demand. For in the 1920s, I was a modern young man, I guess, and I had read Chekhov and Kafka and Hemingway, Mansfield and Joyce, who had all dispensed with formula plots and found better ways. In these postmodernist years, I suppose the ways they found may look commonplace, or even anachronistic, but in the '20s, believe me, they were revelation. In place of winnings and losings, they all dealt in nuances, epiphanies, illuminations. Often nobody won and nobody lost. Often there was no resolution, only a kind of revealing—sometimes sudden; sometimes, as in Chekhov, as gradual as a very slow dawn. And sometimes, as in Kafka, stories never ended at all—they just raveled away like dreams that you lose even while you try to hang on to them.

My distaste for that lecture stemmed partly from the fact that he was commercial, and I was above *that*; partly from his carpenter's-rule method, but most of all—I finally understood—from the fact that he had nothing *but* method. He wrote from an unvarying blueprint; he pulled prepackaged, frivolous surprises out of his sleeve to elicit a gee-whiz response from the reader. There was no fire in his belly, there was no passion or vision or doubt in his mind, no penetration or challenge in what he wrote. He illuminated nothing; he opened no windows; he left no worm of wonder working in his reader's mind. He had nothing to say, in other words, and nothing to ask, beyond the questions to which he had just precooked the answers. He was a mechanic. The writers I admired and still admire were not carpenters, but more like sculptors. Their art was and is a real probing of real and troubling human confusions. They spurned replicas; they despised commercialized entertainment. They were after the mystery implicit in the stone.

By now I'm prepared to guess that *any* method that lets a reader lay bare any moment of that mystery is legitimate. Skill is whatever works. Different skills will work for different writers and upon different readers, but any skill must, I think, work *toward* something. We're not creating machines that are going to do nothing but run. They gotta *make* something. Moreover, the eye, I think, is not a copier. It must add something to what it sees. The late Donald Barthelme, who wrote very, very short stories, confessed that he was in love with fragments, and he was probably speaking his mind pretty truly. But he forgot to say that he adds something to his fragments, and that the best of them are more than fragments—they're illuminations. One page, or six hundred? A fiction is more than a well-carpentered entertainment. It's also more than the mirror in the roadway that Stendhal said it was. Because a good writer isn't really a mirror. He's a lens. One mirror is like another mirror—a mechanical reflector. But a lens may be anything from what you have in your Instamatic to what makes you handle your Hasselblad with reverence.

Ultimately, I think there's no escaping the fact that fiction is only as good as the person who makes it. It sees only with the clarity that he's capable of, and it perpetuates all of his astigmatisms. It should make me nervous, and it does, to talk about my own writing, when both the writing I talk about and the things I say about it may be revealing my own astigmatisms, of which I am unaware. It sounds almost as if I were afraid of being found out, as if there are secrets in there—that I'm disguising myself behind a mask in order to make statements that are my own statements. Or else perhaps that my novels are all romans à clef, or confessions or something of the kind, and that there are keys to them, which should not be revealed. All of which I think is somewhat irritating and somewhat nonsensical. No novel, even one that's meant to be autobiographical, can be read in so naively literal a fashion as that.

Writers are a little more cunning than their credulous readers suppose. We're all practiced shape-shifters and ventriloquists; we can assume shapes and speak in voices not our own. We all have to have in some degree what Keats called "negative capability," that capacity to inhabit a skin not your own. What Shakespeare, for instance, had in incomparable degrees; nobody has ever had it more. He could speak with total persuasiveness out of the mouth of Hotspur or Shylock, Iago or Hamlet or Juliet. Faulkner, I think, too, had it supremely. You couldn't possibly make any kind of autobiographical reconstruction of Faulkner's life from his fictions any more than you can reconstruct Shakespeare—as people have always tried to do, ever since he died—from his plays. Almost all of us have some of that capacity. Some don't use it, or use it very little. If you look at the fictions of—oh, for three—Hemingway; Thomas Wolfe—the first Thomas Wolfe; Katherine Anne Porter—you keep encountering these characters who haunt the thing, like recurring clones of their authors. The differences between those extremes of objectivity and subjectivity are obvious but not really critical. Some writers want to expose themselves; some want to hide themselves; some want to efface themselves. Some who appear to expose themselves are distorting themselves for sneaky reasons of their own. There's more than one way to impose order on your personal chaos. But since good writers write what is important to them, they're bound to be in there somewhere, as participants or as observers or as ombudsmen or as something.

I think if you think about it, you will recall that there are not so many autobiographies by fiction writers. Unlike soldiers or statesmen, they don't get to a certain age and feel that they have to rush to put it all down for posterity. The reason may be that most fiction writers have already written their autobiographies piecemeal, overtly or covertly, and they go on doing so every working day. Somebody said to me once, "I envy you—how nice it must be to be able to write your life instead of having to live it." He had it a little bit wrong. It isn't a substitution; it's a succession. You live it first, and then you write it. Once you have written it, though, or parts of it, even in disguise or modulated form, you find that you've just about used it up as autobiographical principal.

If there is a sense in which every piece of fiction is autobiographical, it's just as true, I think, that every autobiography is to some extent a fiction. A couple of years ago I had the disturbing experience of having to write a short autobiography for a reference book, and while I was doing it I noticed three things: one was the difficulty of getting my precious life into ten thousand words—it bothered me a great deal; the second was that I constantly had the feeling that I'd written all this before; and the third was that on every page I had to restrain myself to keep from fixing it. I went around and around myself like a fussy mother fixing her fifteen-year-old up for her first formal dance. I was running a kind of sack race, leg-bound by these facts that I didn't want to be leg-bound by, whereas, when I had rendered some of that same experience earlier, as fiction, I could be as cavalier with it as I wanted, because where the fiction called for some kind of change, I could make it. I wasn't writing history. In the interest of general truthfulness I wanted all this to be true, but I could fix it to be truer than it had been in fact. In an autobiography, I couldn't. And I don't know which version is truer, when you come right down to it. They're different, but they're both attempts, of a kind, at truth. As an example of how close fiction and autobiography sometimes are—you might know one of Philip Roth's Zuckerman books, called *The Facts*, which is not the facts at all. The book purports to give the true dope on the life of Philip Roth, as distinguished from the life of his stooge, Zuckerman, but in *The Facts*, Zuckerman, the fiction, enters unbidden—or not quite unbidden, really invited when it comes down to it—and from the sidelines he emits these challenges and Bronx cheers and snorts of disdain while his author goes through the charade of telling his life story. *The Facts* is as surely a novel posing as an autobiography as *Zuckerman Unbound* is an autobiography masquerading as a novel.

In his *Education*, Henry Adams wrote, "Chaos is the law of nature; order is the dream of man." Both fiction and autobiography attempt, it seems to me, to impose order upon the only life that any of us knows, which is our own. Once, at a literary meeting, I heard someone ask John Cheever why he wrote—one of those author-felling questions that comes from the audience sometimes. But he replied without hesitation, "To try to make sense of my life." Which is the best answer I could think of. The life we all live is to many degrees and in many ways amateurish and accidental. It begins in accident and proceeds by trial and error toward dubious ends. That's the law of nature. The dream of man won't accept what nature hands us. We have to tinker with it, the way I was tinkering with my autobiography. Trying to give it purpose, direction, and meaning—or if you're of another set of mind, trying to prove that it doesn't have any purpose, set, or meaning—either way, we can't leave it alone. The unexamined life, as the wise Greek said, is not worth living. We *have* to examine it, if only to persuade ourselves that we matter and are in control, or that we at least are aware of what's being done to us.

Autobiography and fiction are variant means to the same end, and neither one should be wrapped in any straitjacket of method. The method becomes paramount only when it's an end in itself and begins to impose its structure on the matter—when it's a formula for arriving at prepackaged answers and evading the real questions. The guts of any significant fiction or autobiography, I think, is an anguished question. The true art of fiction, in which I include autobiography, involves putting that question within a plausible context of order. When we invent fictional characters, as when we invent gods, we generally invent them in our own image, and in any case we create the unknown out of the materials of the known. The worlds that novelists create, even those fantasy worlds of forward or backward time or space, are made out of the details of the world we know. Try to think of a new color, for instance. Invention and method have to fuse. The writer may play games of distortion, double exposure, deliberately blurred focus—he may focus upon himself focusing, as John Barth and others have done when they try to write fiction out of the act of writing fiction, make a story out of writing a story. And ingenious as that often is, it gets a little Alexandrian for my taste, I guess. I do believe the real world exists and that literature is the imitation of life, and I like to keep my categories at least recognizable. Sleight of hand, however clever, is not enough, and distortion can be a method with real dangers in it, I think.

Thus, the admirable artist Flannery O'Connor said that she dealt in the grotesque because when dealing with the hard of hearing one had to shout. That remark rather offends me as a reader; I don't think I'm hard of hearing. And anyway, with the truly deaf, shouting doesn't help; it only confuses and annoys and leads to arguments. I like O'Connor's stories, which kind of rise out of her unconscious, better than her justification of them. Because her justification of them seems to me doctrinaire. Having no such spiritual convictions as she had, I have to make do with spiritual uncertainties. And having, besides, a temperamental aversion to the hyperboles of distortion, I have had to clarify the only life I know the only way I know how. My life challenged me to make sense of it, and I made fictions. But I wanted the fictions to be recognizable and true to the ordinary perception, not necessarily to the deaf. And I thought I could best achieve that aim with a method that was direct, and undistorted, and what is sometimes called, I think falsely, "realistic." Ansel Adams, the late, great photographer, trying to explain what his photographs were about, borrowed a word from his idol, Stieglitz—the word "equivalent." The photographic image is an *equivalent* of the feeling the artist had when he took the picture—a form of transferable currency. I will accept that notion for fiction, too. And like Adams and Edward Weston and Imogen Cunningham and others of that San Francisco f/64 group, I prefer to avoid the double exposures, the imitation of painting, the tricky lighting, the artful compositions, and rely insofar as I can on found objects, natural lighting, and the clear statement of the lens, however good the lens is. Literature is a function of temperament, and thank God there are many temperaments, many kinds, and therefore many kinds of writers. I can speak only for my own, and after considerable acquaintance I have determined that my temperament is quiet, receptive, skeptical, and watchful.

I don't like big, noisy scenes, in fiction or in life. I avoid riots and mass meetings. It would embarrass me to chase fire engines. I have a hard enough time making sense out of what my life hands me, without going out hunting more exciting events.

About thirty years ago, in London, I got into a discussion with Martha Gellhorn, whom some of you may remember as Hemingway's third wife, a journalist, and a very able one. She told me with admirable frankness that though I wrote like a bird, I didn't write about anything that interested her. She had just returned from reporting some of those very early, ugly events in the Sinai Desert, in the Gulf of Aqaba. And she thought I ought to go down there, or somewhere like it, somewhere where something was *happening*, so that I could apply my talents to subjects worthy of them. And I'm afraid I offended her by saying that I thought that would be a kind of slumming. Not for her, because she was a journalist, that was her business, but for me, a fiction writer. I didn't think then and I don't think now that going out and committing experience in order to be able to write about it is any good way to make sense of my life. Unless I was irresistibly drawn to the Israeli-Arab conflict, unless I had some personal stake in it, unless I had some way of working it out and trying to bring it to an end, I thought that I ought, out of sheer sympathy, to leave that desert to the people whose commitments led them to shed their blood there.

As with excitement and violence, so with self-conscious innovation. One observable fact about "experimental writing," so-called, is that it often turns out to be a belated imitation of James Joyce. Another is that, like biological mutations, experimental forms and manners seldom survive. As long as I'm saying what doesn't interest me, I might as well fill out the list: as I wouldn't be tempted to exploit the battles or troubles of strangers for my own purposes, or play innovator for the sake of being in on the latest fad, so I haven't

ever been driven to thump what H. L. Mencken called "the bou-
boisie," or foam in rage at the middlebrows, or speak in thunder
on the morning headlines. Not in fiction; fiction's too important to
be abused that way. In fiction, I think we should have no agenda
except to try to be truthful. The shouters in thunder can roar from
their podiums and pulpits; I squeak from my corner. They speak to
the deaf, but it takes good ears to hear me. For I want to be part of
the common sound, a not-too-dominating element of the ambient
noise.

I'm old enough to have watched a lot of bright innovations
and passionate causes fade out as fads, just as in my childhood I
watched a lot of hopeful short-grass homesteaders fade out and
disappear before the hot winds and the drought. My family was
among them. We turned tail and disappeared. And I never got
over the faint, residual shame of quitting. If we hadn't quit, I'd be
stuck up there in the boondocks. I wouldn't have been very good,
and yet there is a kind of shame in it. I admired the stickers, and
I still do. And perhaps that is why, if I had the capacity to wish
myself into any novelist who ever wrote, or any writer who ever
wrote, I would be much more likely to pick, let us say, Henry
Fielding's *Tom Jones*—I'd rather be the author of *Tom Jones* than
of Lyly's *Euphues*, or if you want to make the comparison a little
fairer, Sterne's *Tristram Shandy*, which is an experimental novel
of a very early kind. Funny too, but lesser somehow, slighter.
Those attitudes I've grown into pretty slowly. I started as I've just
said: with the revolutionary and iconoclastic attitudes of the '20s,
a time when I was in college. I vorted with the Vorticists and
imaged with the Imagists. If I'd been able to get to Paris, I would
have babbled with the Dadaists, I suppose, in the direction of total
intellectual, artistic, and emotional disaffiliation. But there was
one trouble: I'd grown up a migrant, without history, tradition, or

extended family, in remote backwaters of the West. I never saw a water closet or a lawn till I was eleven years old. I never met a person with my surname, apart from my parents and brother, till I was past thirty years old. I never knew, and don't know now, the first names of three of my grandparents. My family either didn't tell me about any of that or couldn't have; neither of my parents had finished grade school, and their uprooting was the cause of mine. My mother was sympathetic and supportive and, I think, a saint, but she hadn't the tools to help me in many of the ways that I thought I needed help.

And so, though I was susceptible to the dialectic of those who declared their independence of custom and tradition and the dead hand of the past, I had no tradition to declare myself independent of, and I never felt the dead hand of the past in my life. If the truth were told, and it now is, I was always hungry to feel that hand on my head. It belonged to some socially or intellectually or historically or literarily cohesive group, some tribe, some culture, some recognizable and persistent offshoot of Western civilization. If I revolted—and I had all the appropriate temptations—I had to revolt away from what I was, and that meant towards something else—tradition, cultural memory, shared experience, order. Even my prose felt the pull of agreed-upon grammar and syntax. I found it hard to write in nonsentences. Eventually, inevitably, I was drawn to what I most needed.

I've been trying to make some kind of natural chaos into human order, trying to make sense of an ordinary American life for a long time now—more than fifty years in print. The West in which I have spent most of my life is not simply a retarded culture, though it once was. It's also a different culture from that of the literary capitals; a different culture with different drives and assumptions and prides and avenues of opportunity. School and college do sandpaper the roughness of the frontier off a little, but the frontier leaves its tracks. My first fifteen years were migrant and deprived; my next fifteen, aspiring and academic and literary and deprived; and my last fifty-odd, academic and literary and not quite so deprived. That's progress, I suppose, of a sort. But I'm still the person my first fifteen years made me.

Without consciously intending to, I've written my life. *The Big Rock Candy Mountain* and *Wolf Willow* cover the years of frontier transience and the Dakotas, Washington, Saskatchewan, Montana, Utah, and Nevada. *The Preacher and the Slave*, about the IWW martyr Joe Hill, and *Recapitulation*, one of those growing-up-in-the-'20s novels, utilize the milieu of Salt Lake City, where I attended high school and college. About that place I've also written histories, biographies, essays, and short stories. My forty-five years in California are reflected in *A Shooting Star*, *The Spectator Bird*, *All the Little Live Things*, some stories, *Angle of Repose*—all of them utilizing houses and communities we lived in, and all of them inevitably revealing some fragments of myself. *Angle of Repose* does escape the personal to some extent—I borrowed a set of ancestors, entire. But, because I chose to tell that story in the first person, a lot of people have mistakenly recognized me in Lyman Ward's wheelchair.

Of all the books I ever wrote, the latest one, latest novel—*Crossing to Safety*—is in some ways the most personal. It is, in fact, deliberately close to my experience, opinions, and feelings, which are refracted through a narrator not too much different from myself. If *The Big Rock Candy Mountain* was an exorcism, and it was, *Crossing to Safety* is an attempt to understand and make sense of an important relationship in the lives of my wife and myself, a friendship that was rich and rewarding, but that left us fumbling for meanings and unsure of our emotional ground. I could also say, though I wouldn't press this, that it's an attempt to make the commonplace memorable, to communicate through the story of essentially uninflected lives all the pain, anguish, confusion, affection, sacrifice, the spontaneous pleasures and the unanticipated catastrophes of the kind of living that most of us experience. It was a risky book to set before a reading public accustomed to spicier fare—there isn't a murder, a divorce, an illicit weekend, a gun, a liaison, a drug dream, a hot sex scene, even a wild party in it. It deals with academics, who by definition are tepid and undramatic.

Two young couples meet in the Depression in Madison, Wisconsin. One pair is rich, well-endowed, well-connected, and ambitious. The second is poor, orphaned, unconnected, and ambitious. The two men face similar problems, similar crises of promotion and tenure, which are endemic in the academic atmosphere; the wives are both pregnant. Nothing there to strain the acting powers of Clint Eastwood. Over the course of thirty years, these couples have children, suffer disappointment and illness, make do, put one foot after the other, survive, and are bent but not broken by their experiences. Very different in their personalities, they remain close friends, as some people do. They don't always approve of one another; in fact, all three of the others have difficulty accepting the dominating personality of Charity Lang. But friendship outlasts disapproval, irritation, and matriarchal rigor. At the end of the book, and for that matter, at the beginning, since the front-stage action takes only a day, Charity is on her way out of the lives that she loved and supported and dominated, and the others are left to survive, each according to his or her individual nature and condition, relying on whatever it is that, in a long life, they would not part with. The themes of the novel are love, friendship, and survival. The villains are willfulness, polio, cancer, and blind chance. The tensions are the tensions between and among people who love each other at least as much as they resent each other and resist each other. It's all very quiet. I intended it to be true. I wrote my guts out trying to make it as moving on the page as it had been to me while I was living and reliving it.

My reason for writing that novel was not literary in the usual sense at all. We once had such friends as Sid and Charity Lang, and I tried to put them on the page without distortion, as far as I could do it—without exaggeration or heightening—because I kept trying, even after they were both dead, to understand them. I wanted to work out iconically the deepest and most troubling relationship of our lives and, at the same time, the most rewarding. I wanted to comprehend how a woman as charming as Charity Lang, a woman with every grace and every opportunity—affectionate, generous, thoughtful, intending only good—could at the same time be a domineering matriarch, a willful putter-downer of her husband, a tyrant sometimes to the children whose every first tooth and first disease she lovingly preserved in the family records, a woman who could say in anguish at the end, "My God, I've done so much harm," when all she had intended was affection and help. I wanted to understand how it might have been to be Charity's husband, by what combination of love, forgiveness, weakness, and self-deception Sid Lang could have submitted to a lifetime of humiliating henpecking. I knew how it was to be Charity's friend—alternately baffled, angry, and disarmed. Only by writing her straight, as I knew her, could I get a clue on how it felt to be a member of her family.

I suppose I wanted to justify those lives, bring them together, lay their ghosts. And in that effort I wrote very close to memory and fact. I resisted whenever I felt myself wanting to adjust or improve or straighten out. I adopted a narrator who, though not myself, was not unlike me—a Western orphan, upwardly mobile, making his way. I used episodes from our actual experience because, better than any invented episodes, they evoked the quality of our relationship. I reported the scene of Charity's going off to hospital to die exactly as my wife, who was present, reported it to me. I relied on memory for many scenes: the birth of Sally Morgan's child, the sailing mishap on Lake Mendota in Madison, the walking trip in the Green Mountains, the dinner party at which the four of us first became friends.

Nevertheless, I was not running a sack race. I was not tightly bound—as I would have been in a history or biography or autobiography—by explicit facts. I could expand or contract, unify, amplify, or omit according to some interior stabilizer that told me what was right *here*—for this book, for this story—and what was not. What I wrote was a labor of love and bafflement, I suppose, so close to the facts that at first I didn't even intend to publish the book, because I knew everybody would recognize the people in it. But I had made more unconscious changes than I knew, and members of the family themselves helped to persuade me that what I had written was a novel, not a case history or a memoir, and so should be published. I didn't even emerge with any answers, prefabricated or earned. I emerged with as many questions as I had started out with. I still don't understand Charity Lang, or Sid Lang, who loved and endured her. But maybe something has changed. Once I had written them, they achieved a sort of inevitability—there they were in a book, characters made permanent, irrevocably what they were. And even I, who put them in the book, feel them somehow more substantial and less troubling than when they existed only in my life and my memory.

So here we are, back where we began: how to write a story though ignorant or baffled. It takes something that is of real importance to you, something you have brooded about. You try to see it as clearly as you can and to fix it in a transferable equivalent.

All you want in the finished print is the clear statement of the lens, which is yourself, on the subject that has been absorbing your attention. Sure, it's autobiography. Sure, it's fiction. Either way, if you have done it faithfully, it ought to be true.

Morality and Truth in Literature

ROBERT STONE

April 19, 1988

In April of 1987, the writer and critic William Gass published an article in *Harper's Magazine* entitled "Goodness Knows Nothing of Beauty," which toyed with the proposition that art and moral aspiration are mutually distant. Statements of this view very often seem to replicate in their style the kind of cool, amoral elegance they claim for good art. Mr. Gass's piece is not, in this regard, exceptional; it is characterized by paradox, alliteration, and a faintly decadent naughtiness suggestive of intense sophistication. In the end, as such pieces often do, it resolves itself solipsistically; that is, it explains itself away in terms of its own moral and aesthetic definitions. But it is interesting to see this old opposition between art and morality appear again, offered by a commentator who is usually so wise and insightful. "To be a preacher is to bring your sense of sin to the front of the church," says Mr. Gass. "But to be an artist is to give to every mean and ardent,

petty and profound, feature of the soul a glorious godlike shape."
If this means that you get no points in art for good intentions,
no one would argue. But here I find echoes of an old, romantic,
antinomian tendency that goes back at least to Nietzsche. It has
been argued by people as different as Ortega y Gasset and Oscar
Wilde, by Joyce speaking in character as Stephen Dedalus, and by
Shaw during the period when he was writing *Major Barbara*, and,
it now appears, attempting to invent fascism. In this antinomian
vision, morality and art are independent, and even in opposition.
On the right squats morality. It may be imagined as a neo-Gothic
structure: immense, ornate, and sterile. Its self-satisfaction, lack
of imagination, and philistine sentimentality are advertised in its
every plane and line. Architecturally, it resembles the Mormon
tabernacle—the one in downtown Salt Lake City, not the Hollywood one on Santa Monica Boulevard. It contains drear, echoing
silences. And over here, art. Art is nothing but beautiful. Art is
like a black panther. It has the glamour of a desperado. Art is radical, the appealing cousin of crime. Never a dull moment with art.
Morality, in this view, is not only its opposite but also its enemy.
This claim of estrangement between morality and art retains its
currency for an excellent reason: it's fun. It's agreeable for an artist
to imagine himself as a Zarathustran rope dancer balanced against
eternity up in the ozone-thin light, while far below the eunuchs
of the brown temple of morality whine platitudes at each other in
the incense-ridden noonday darkness: "Look before you leap," or
"A stitch in time saves nine."

Let us imagine the novel, for example, freed completely from
moral considerations. What would that be like? It might be like
one of the antinovels Monsieur Robbe-Grillet wrote during the
1950s and '60s. These are novels not only without any moral context but also without characters, plots, beginnings, or endings.

Surely such an exercise in doing *without* something serves to reinforce the idea of its necessity. Is it possible to postulate the idea of a successful novel about people—or about animals for that matter—in which the living of life that exists beyond the signal area of any moral reference points is reflected? What about the comic novel? Let's eliminate at the outset the obviously sentimental or political comedies that have a message at their core. Let's take the work of two writers who have written very funny books and who are not usually thought of as kindly, humanistic sages: William Burroughs and Evelyn Waugh. *Naked Lunch* is the prototypical Burroughs novel and, like all his others, it's full of cruelty. Not just sadism, but cruelty. The element of sci-fi political satire it contains is sometimes advanced as representative of its moral dimension, but I think that's bogus. The moral element in William Burroughs's work is in its very humor. In the grimmest imaginable places—in the grammar of drug addiction, in the violence and treachery of the addict's world—Burroughs finds laughter. The laughter itself is a primary moral response. Laughter represents a rebellion against chaos, a rejection of evil, and an affirmation of balance and soundness. One can see this principle at work in the way laughter undermines super-serious attempts at self-consciously wicked sex. I was once given a description of a waterfront S&M joint that presented itself as the meanest saloon on earth. There was a dress code, and patrons were expected to present nothing less than a grim mask of depravity to any observer. There were two house rules, according to my informant: no rugby shirts and no laughing. We must assume that the people who run places like that know what they're doing.

Evelyn Waugh seems to have been lacking in all the qualities we philanthropists find congenial. A bully, a coward, a fascist, a despiser of minorities and the poor, a groveler before the rich and powerful, Waugh was surely one of the worst human beings ever to become a major novelist. But paradoxically, his life and work provide us with a ringing confirmation of serious fiction's dependence on morality. By borrowing—spuriously or otherwise, it doesn't matter—the certainties of Catholicism, he was able to infuse his best work with the moral center that makes it great. The worldly lives described in *Men at Arms* and *Brideshead Revisited* are constantly being measured against a rigorous, neo-Jansenist Christianity. In these books, the invisible world becomes the real one, and its meanings constitute the truth that underlies the confusion of desires in which the characters struggle. Gass's essay starts by having us ask ourselves whether we'd rescue an infant or a Botticelli painting if we saw both being washed out to sea and could only salvage one. The Botticelli's a masterpiece; the baby's only a potential human being. After prescribing us this brisk antinomian exercise, he commences to deflate his own balloon by running it onto the thorns of common sense. He refers to the historical struggle against censorship as though it had somehow established art's essentially amoral character, and then admits that each censoring hierarchy was reacting to whatever inadequacies of its moral system were challenged by the work in question. He reminds us that good books can be written by bad people. Then he ends with a truism to the effect that propaganda can't justify bad art or bad writing.

There are few statements in the essay that Gass does not obviate or contradict in the next paragraph, but there is one that stays— unforesworn and unqualified—in my recollection. He refers to Keats's identification of beauty with truth and vice versa as "a fatuous little motto." I think this is being unkind to a perfectly nice axiom; perhaps it is a hasty judgment. Surely we should meditate for a moment on Keats's appealing sentiment. Is it true? Concerning life, that is a question we cannot finally answer. I think it tends to be true. The explanation at the core of one of nature's mysteries is often edifying. Job cuts through to the substance of this when he questions the munificence of God. In the end he learns that God is worshipful, that God's majesty and holiness suffuse the universe. This is what the medieval mystic Julian of Norwich was referring to when she wrote, "All shall be well, and all shall be well, and all manner of thing shall be well." In terms of Western tradition, it should be true that truth is beauty. Even if you take God out of it, the grimaced principles of existence have their symmetry. All the same, there can be a hundred different explanations for things, every one of them beautiful, and none of them true. But isn't art always true? Aren't truth and beauty very nearly the same? Surely every aesthetic response entails recognition. What standard do we hold up to art other than things themselves? And what do we require from art, if not a reflection of things—of our lives in all their variety?

We are, in the Western world, what the Muslims call "people of a book." Our prototypical book has been the Bible, regardless of whether we are believers or whether we were brought up by believers. After centuries of being Christians and Jews, our context and perceptions continue to be conditioned by the Bible's narratives. It's hard to overestimate its impact on our civilization and on our language. The novel came into existence with the rise of literacy and mass readership, and the greatest vehicle of mass literacy in the English-speaking world has been the King James Bible, the great primer.

The Bible is unique among religious books due to the relationship it defines between God and mankind, and in the view it takes of human life. The narratives about people in the books of the Bible are thought to *mean* something; they are thought to be significant. This implies that the corporeal world in which people live is not an illusion to be overcome, or a shadowland reflecting the void, but an instrument of God's will. For centuries we have been reflecting on peculiar things like why Esau was disinherited and how Isaac could have been ready to sacrifice his son, asking ourselves, "What does this mean? What is at the heart of this strange story? What can I learn from it? How does it bear on *my* situation?" All our philosophies of history descend from the assumptions bequeathed by our scriptures, in that they profess to detect informing principles at the heart of human events: Life matters. Lives matter. Earthly human history is the arena in which the universe acts out its consciousness of itself, displaying its nature as creation. Human annals become charged; they become an entity— history. History, then, is perceived as a rational process, the unfolding of a design, something with a dynamic to be uncovered. Stories explain the nature of things. Any fictional work of serious intent argues for the significance of its history. A reader holds the characters in judgment, investing sympathy or withholding it, always alert to recognition, hoping to see his lonely state reflected across time, space, and circumstance. How then can fiction ever be a process independent of morality? To be so, it would have to be composed of something other than language.

There is no brown temple where morality resides. There is no high wire above where the artist whirls in freedom. If there's a wire, it's the wire we're all on out here—the one we live on—with only each other for company. Our having each other is both the good news and the bad. We deceive ourselves, we contemporary people, if we imagine that beneath our feet there's a great, sound structure, a vast warehouse called "civilization" chockablock with boring, reliable truths and insights. Around us there is only deep space. Out here, where we all live with each other, it's mostly impromptu. Right-mindedness is cheap, but *goodness*? William Gass need not worry about its coming between ourselves and our pleasures.

Most journalists who worked in Vietnam during the war were oppressed by the extreme difficulty of translating what they saw into words. It was not necessarily that it was so uniquely horrible; it was that the brutality and confusion one experienced seemed to lose something when rendered into language. Somehow, describing the situation so that it could be set up in columns of type always seemed to be cleaning it up. I once pondered this process, and a moment of illumination, or so it seemed, struck me: We are forever cleaning up our act. Not only in describing ourselves but also in *imagining* ourselves. We project a self-image that is considerably idealized. In our relationships with other people, we conventionalize ourselves so as not to frighten them with our primary process. And just as we, individually, cultivate elevated images of ourselves, so we collectively conspire—as nations, peoples, as humankind—to create a fictional exemplar of our collective selves, our selves as we have agreed to imagine ourselves.

But this is not the whole story. Though we are only what we are, we have an amazing ability to extend, to transcend the grimmest of circumstances. Moments occur when we amaze each other with acts of hope, acts of courage, that can make one proud to be human. The fact is that we absolutely require the elevated image of ourselves that we indulge. If we did not idealize ourselves, if we accepted only the reality of ourselves as we are most of the time, we would never be capable of extending ourselves in the ways that are required of us. "Things are in the saddle," Emerson said, "and ride mankind." "Whirl is king." Things happen ruthlessly, without mercy. The elemental force of things bears down on us. From one moment to the next, we hardly know what's going on, let alone what it all means. Civilization and its attendant morality are not massive structures; they're more like notions. And sometimes they can seem very distant notions. They can be blown away in a second. In the worst of times, we often look for them in vain. Sometimes the morality to which we publicly subscribe appears so alien to our actual behavior that it seems to emanate from some other sphere. One might call it a fiction. But it's a fiction that we most urgently require. It is much more difficult to act well than we are ready to admit. It can be extremely hard to act *sensibly*, let alone well. Storytelling is not a luxury to humanity; it's almost as necessary as bread. We cannot imagine ourselves without it, because the self is a story. The perception each of us has of his own brief, transient passage through things is also a kind of fiction, not because its matter is necessarily untrue, but because we tend to shape it to suit our own needs. We tell ourselves our own stories, selectively, in order to keep our sense of self intact. As dreams are to waking life, so fiction is to reality. The brain can't function without clearing its circuits during sleep, nor can we contemplate and analyze our situations without living some of the time in the world of imagination, sorting and refining the random promiscuity of events. If the practice of fiction is inextricably linked with concerns of morality, what is there to say about the writer's responsibility? The writer's responsibility, it seems to me, consists in writing well and truly—to use a Hemingway-esque locution. The writer who betrays his calling is a writer who, either for commercial or political reasons, vulgarizes his own perception and his rendering of it. Meretricious writing tries to conventionalize what it describes in order to make it safer and easier to take. It may do this to conform to a political agenda that is seen as somehow more important than mere literary considerations, or under commercial pressures to appeal to the limitations of a mass audience. The effect of conventionalized, vulgarized writing is pernicious. Fiction is an act against loneliness, an appeal to community, a bet on the possibility of spanning the gulf that separates one human being from another. It must understand and illustrate the varieties of the human condition in order to bring more of that condition into the light of conscious insight. It is part of the process that expands human self-knowledge. Meretricious fiction does the opposite of what fiction is supposed to do. The reassurances it offers are superficial and empty. It presents a reality that is limited by its own impoverishment, and as a result it increases each individual's loneliness and isolation. In the absence of honest storytelling, people are abandoned to the beating of their own hearts. Without it, the burden of life is lonelier than it need be. The moral imperative of fiction provides no excuse for smug moralizing, religiosity, or propaganda; on the contrary, it forbids them. Nor does it require that every writer equip his work with some edifying message advertising progress, brotherhood, and light. It does not require a writer to be a good man—only a good wizard.

Above all, what I wish to argue is that the laws of both language and art impose choices that are unavoidably moral. The first law of heaven is that nothing is free. This is the law that requires the artist to make decisions constantly—to choose between symmetry or asymmetry, restraint or excess, balance or imbalance. Because this law is ruthlessly self-enforcing in art, the quality of the artist's work will depend on his making the right decisions. The same law operates the scales that the blindfolded woman in the courthouse holds. Artistic quality is related to justice. Grammar is related to logic, the engine of conscience. Language is always morally weighted. Nothing is free. Again and again it seems to me I have come up against that principle. Political situations have always been attractive to me as subject matter, and not because I believe that political pathology is necessarily more "important" than private suffering. During times of political upheaval the relationship between external reality and the individual's interior world becomes destabilized. Revolutions, wars, any such upheavals, liberate some people from the prison of the self as they invite others to play out their personal dramas on a larger stage. People caught up in things that transcend the personal forever bring their own needs and desires to bear. They make pleasant and unpleasant discoveries about each other and themselves. The elements of drama descend on ordinary people and ordinary lives.

I wrote my first book after spending a year in the Deep South that happened to coincide with the first sit-ins in the beginning of the struggle for desegregation. It was written during a period of great change in this country—the first half of the 1960s. It centered on the exploitation of electronic media by the extreme right, a phenomenon that we have not put behind us. *A Hall of Mirrors* was not strictly a realistic book, but as young writers will, I put every single thing I thought I knew into it. I gave my characters names with the maximum number of letters because I thought that would make them more substantial. All my quarrels with America went into it. A few years later, working in Vietnam, I found myself witnessing a mistake ten thousand miles long, a mistake on the American scale. Since I believed I had taken America as my subject, I began to write a novel set in Saigon. As it progressed, I realized that the logic of the thing required that everybody make their way back home into the America of the early 1970s. The early to mid-1970s still seem to me in retrospect like a creaky, evil time. A lot of due bills from the parties of the '60s were coming up for presentation. *Dog Soldiers* was my reaction to the period. I went to Central America in 1976 to go scuba diving (while at work on a different novel) and returned several times thereafter. I became acquainted with a few Americans working there. At that time relatively few people in this country knew where Huehuetenango was, and "Managua, Nicaragua" was the title of an old Andrews Sisters song. The Somozas had been running Nicaragua for many years, and they seemed quite secure in their power—at least to my touristic eyes. Everything was quiet there. One day I even semi-crashed a party at the presidential palace, which stood in the middle of what was literally a fallen city. From a distance, downtown Managua looked like a park, it was so green. When one got closer, one could see that the green was that of vegetation growing over the rubble where the center of the city had collapsed on Christmas Eve, 1972. The presidential palace stood unscathed in the middle of the destruction. Around it was a kind of free-fire zone of scrub jungle no one was permitted to enter. The palace stood just beyond the effective mortar distance from the nearest habitation.

I made a few more trips to Central America and I tried to make a point of listening to as many stories as I could. After a while the stories began to form a pattern that conformed to my sense of Mesoamerica's history. This band of republics seemed placed by its gods in a very fateful situation. They seemed to have drawn the most violent conquistadors and the most fanatical inquisitors. On arrival, the Spaniards had found holy wells of human sacrifice. There, racial and social oppression had always been most severe. The fertile soil of the place seemed to bring forth things to provoke the appetite rather than things to nourish—baubles and rich toys, plantation crops for your sweet tooth or for your head. These lands were yoked to labor-intensive, high-profit products—bananas, of course, and coffee, chocolate, tobacco, chicle, emeralds, marijuana, cocaine. And since my subject was again America, and the United States had been involved in Latin America for so long, by the time I got back to the States I had decided to put down the book I was writing and begin a new one, which became my third novel, *A Flag for Sunrise*.

In my view, *Children of Light*, a book about the movies that I published in 1986, is also political. The process that goes into creating American movies is loaded with examples of how America works. People in the film industry who see *Children of Light* as an attack on moviemaking apparently fail to see how movie-struck and reverent it really is. I do not claim to know much more about novels than the writing of them, but I cannot imagine one set in the breathing world that lacks any moral valence. In the course of wringing a few novels out from our fin-de-siècle, late-imperial scene, I have never been able to escape my sense of humanity try-ing, with difficulty, to raise itself in order not to fail. I insist on disputing William Gass's claim that goodness knows nothing of beauty. Nor do I believe that, in writing his excellent fiction and lucid criticism, he practices the dehumanized art celebrated years ago by Ortega y Gasset, echoes of which seem to appear in his essay. And just as it's possible to avoid standards of human action in novels about people, it's difficult to avoid politics. But if a nov-elist openly accepts that his work must necessarily contain moral and political dimensions, what responsibilities does he take on? He assumes, above all, the responsibility to understand. The novel that admits to a political dimension requires a knowledge—legiti-mately or illegitimately acquired, intuitive or empirical—of the situation that is its subject. Political commitment is not required, although eventually most authors maneuver themselves into it. I think the key is to establish the connection between political forces and individual lives. The questions an author needs to address are: How do social and political forces condition individual lives? How do the personal qualities of the players condition their political direction? An author has to cast the net of his sympathies fairly wide. He should be able to imagine his way into the personas of many different people, who have different ways of thinking and believing. The aspiring, overtly political novelist might spend a little time every morning meditating on the interior life of Gen-eral Noriega, a man who actually exists. As far as political satire goes, remember that the best satire requires a certain subversive sympathy for one's subject. The writer must remember the first law of heaven: nothing is free. Commitment can be useful because it brings a degree of passion to bear, but it's also dangerous. To be the contented partisan of one side or another, one has to sell something. However, because so much of serious politics in this century consists of violence, this can be a morally enervating exercise. Moral enervation is bad for writers.

Above all, a writer must not sentimentalize. He must remember that sentimentality is the great enemy of genuine sentiment. I believe that it is impossible for any novelist to find a subject other than the transitory nature of moral perception. The most important thing about people is the difficulty they have in identifying and acting upon the right. The world is full of illusion. We carry nemeses inside us. But we are not excused.

Years ago, a whimsical friend of mine made up a little ditty that, for me, sums up the backward-and-forward, tragicomical nature of humanity's march. It's a highly moral little ditty, and it may contain the essence of every work of serious literature ever written. It goes like this: *Of offering more than what we can deliver, we have a bad habit, it is true. But we have to offer more than what we can deliver to be able to deliver what we do.*

What Is Art For?

JEANETTE WINTERSON

November 9, 2000

An American lady visiting Paris in 1913 asked Ezra Pound what he thought art was for. And Pound said, "Ask me what a rosebush is for." Had the American lady been a literalist, she might have begun to talk of rose oil, of cut flowers, of specialist nurseries, of formal gardens, of bees. It is true that rosebushes have commercial uses *and* decorative uses; they provide a living for some, pleasure for others, and pollen for bees everywhere. If we were proceeding on strictly functional principles, and deciding what should or shouldn't be taken aboard a new Noah's ark, I think we would take rosebushes. A case can be made for rosebushes.

But what about art? Can a case be made for art? And where would we begin? Money won't help us, for though we know that huge sums are traded on the art market, and that some writers, painters, and musicians are very wealthy, we sense that money is not the justification of art. And we know that money tells us much less about art than it does about real estate or automobiles. A price tag on a painting will tell me how much it costs, but not how much it is worth. A six-figure sum advanced to a writer is no gauge of how fine his or her book will be. Michelangelo had *five* palaces, and I think we'd all agree he was pretty good at his job, but van Gogh died a pauper, and so did Mozart. And nobody ever said, "When I grow up, I want to be an artist and make lots of *money!*" And nobody ever said, "Books! That's where the *big* money is!" Well, maybe the guys at Amazon did (for reasons that have now become clear—JW, 2014).

No, money won't answer the lady's question. And neither will some vague talk about education or moral sense. Art isn't there to do the job of high schools or churches, and the way we read to pass exams isn't the way we read for pleasure. And art is an unreliable instructor when it comes to morals. Could we recommend *Madame Bovary* to a young woman unhappy in her marriage? Not if our intention was to keep her in it. This example gives us a clue as to why, at various times, art is condemned by churchmen and senators as immoral. America banned James Joyce's *Ulysses* on the grounds that it undermined the American way. Hemingway's *The Sun Also Rises* was for a time banned in Boston. My own book *Oranges Are Not the Only Fruit* has been banned in several states.

Everybody knows that the Ayatollah burned Salman Rushdie's *Satanic Verses* and that Franco refused to allow Picasso's *Guernica* to be exhibited in Spain. But on the other hand, we know, too, how effective art has been at communicating the Christian message— that in pictures and music particularly, we have an iconography of tremendous power and feeling. You don't need to believe in God to be moved by Bach's *Passions* or Handel's *Messiah*. You can be an out-and-out humanist and still feel the strange power of faith when you look at Caravaggio's *Matthew Killed*, or *Matthew Called*.

And yet there are plenty of people who say that the great art of the past leaves them cold, precisely because it is so caught up in religion. They don't want to look at crucified Christs and gleaming Madonnas, and they hate what they call "religious music."

This kind of attitude misses the point and is no better than banning or burning the stuff. The fact is that the purpose of art is not educative or moral or religious for the simple reason that the best art is the art that lasts, and the art that lasts outlasts whatever morals or theories or interpretations of faith were so important— life-and-death important—when the art was first made. We don't look at Caravaggios now because we want to return to the life of simple piety envisaged by the cardinal who commissioned them. We look at them because that wild, strange dark and light still moves us, still makes us puzzle over what it means to be human. We don't read Henry James because American society is still like his books—we read his books because they contain some truths about us that don't date. One of the things that art teaches us is to look past what's period into what's permanent. The time and the place is history, but the feeling is now.

So I'm going to try to answer this question not once or twice, but four times over. It's no good going at art as evolutionary or not evolutionary, as entertainment, as pleasure, as culture, as social indicator. There are more circles to these arguments than in Dante's Hell. I'm going to be simple. And I'm going to start at the beginning, in a very straightforward way: art gives us a sense of ourselves.

I was brought up poor, in a mill town, in the north of England. I was adopted, so my identity was in question at birth. "Who is she?" could only be answered by "We don't know."

My new parents were working class, suspicious of education, and deeply religious. I was targeted for marriage and the missionary field. The book I was given to read was the Bible. Everything else was first vetted by my mother, whose argument against books ran something like, "The trouble with a book is that you never know what's in it until it's too late." Fortunately for me, there was a copy of Malory's *Le Morte d'Arthur* in the house, an ancient, crumbling text left over in a box from a dead uncle. In those stories of Lancelot, Sir Percival, Guinevere, and Morgana Le Fey, I found an escape hatch, that is, a small door to another world. My pleasure, as I tunneled through, taught me my first lesson about myself: I am the kind of person who has need of another world.

I began to smuggle books in and out of the house, usually in my knickers. Anyone with a single bed, standard size, and a collection of paperbacks, standard size, will discover that seventy-seven can be accommodated, per layer, under the mattress. As my collection grew, I began to worry that my mother might notice that her daughter's bed was rising visibly. One day she did. But that was not yet. Meanwhile, against the hymn singing and the miracles, against the poverty and the lack, I was growing a self inside myself that could not be controlled by my parents or my environment. One of the reasons why tyrants hate books, from Hitler to the Ayatollah, is not so much for what they contain, though that is the usual indictment against them, but what they stand for. Church, state, and media have no powers over the private dialogue between a book and its reader. Reading is an act of free will.

A pamphleteer by temperament, my mother knew that sedition and controversy are fired by printed matter. It was because she knew the power of books that she avoided them, countering any influence she suspected with exhortations of her own pasted about the house. The strange thing is that while there were only six books in our house, not counting the ones under the mattress, we lived in a world of print. There were colored cards stuck behind the lights and pinned under the coat hooks. Mine said, "Think of

God, not the dog." In the kitchen, on a loaf wrapper, my mother had written, "Man shall not live by bread alone." In the outside toilet, those who stood up read, "Linger not at the Lord's business," while those who sat down read, "He shall melt thy bowels like wax." It was not as bad as it sounds. My mother was having trouble with her movements, which I suspect was connected to the loaf of white sliced we couldn't live by. It was quite normal for me to find a little sermon in my packed lunch or a few Bible verses, with commentary, shoved inside my hockey boots. Fed words, and shod with them, words became clues. I hunted them down, knowing they would tell me something about which I knew very little—myself. Who am I?

My mother suspected me of harboring print. Library books that were vetted and returned never worried her. It was close association she feared—that a book might fall into my hands and stay there. It never occurred to her that *I* fell into the books, that I put myself inside them for safekeeping. One night, when I was sleeping closer to the ceiling than to the floor, my mother realized the awful truth, and pulling out a corner of D. H. Lawrence, threw the books one by one into the yard and burned them. Not all of them. I had started to shift some of my hoard to a friend's house, and I still have some of those early books, bound in plastic, none of the spines broken.

Soon after that I left home, working at nights and at weekends so that I could continue my education. When I returned to my borrowed room alone, night after night, I felt relief and exuberance, not hardship or exhaustion. There were my books. And I intended to avoid the fate of Thomas Hardy's Jude the Obscure, though a reading of that book was a useful warning. What I wanted did not belong to me by right, and whilst it could not be refused to me in quite the way it was to Jude, we still have subtle punishments for anyone who insists on who they are and what they want. Walled inside the little space marked out for me by family, class, and gender, it was the limitless world of the imagination that made it possible for me to scale the sheer rock face of other people's assumptions. I never thought of myself as a victim or a poor child with too many problems. I thought of myself as Aladdin, Gulliver, Crusoe, Huck Finn, Heathcliff. If my circumstances were a wall, then there was a secret door in the wall and the door was a book. Open it.

We hear a lot of talk today about how difficult it is for young people to develop a sense of self that is more than material crassness. We hear about the divorce rate, the drug problems, the cynicism, the lack of heart. I don't take much notice of any of this. It's always been immensely difficult for anyone to develop a real sense of self. In the past, when social models were tighter and people stayed married, kept their jobs, and didn't stray too much from the same patch, it was easier to hide the plain fact that few of us actually know who we are. Nowadays, not much is hidden. The problems aren't different, or even that much worse, it's just that they're visible. One of the reasons why cults and extreme forms of religion have become so attractive is because they claim to tell us who we are, as individuals and as a society. This is also the reason for the explosion of self-help and improvement books. It's a fast-food format applied to a slow-cook problem. The truth is that a sense of self is really a lifetime of development; it's not quick or easy, but it is possible. And when we start to read literature, look at great art, listen to incredible music, we start to understand life as a quest and ourselves as serious players. You see, art takes us seriously. The time you spend with it is the time it spends with you, one-to-one, no interruptions. And out of that conversation comes a new sense of who you are. As the conversation develops, so do you. And so the old question "Who am I?" begins to shape itself into an answer.

Well then. If we can say to our American lady that art gives us a sense of ourselves, can we also say that it gives us a sense of ourselves in the world? I was traveling to New York earlier this year, and the cover of *Newsweek* caught my attention. The photo showed a group of people of different ages watching something in a trance of grief and disbelief. I wondered what the tragedy was, who was dead, what these people had lost. When I bought the magazine, I found that these people, huddled together out on the street, were watching the NASDAQ crash. The crash wasn't 1929; it wasn't depression, or even recession. It was what happens to a bubble. The people in the photo weren't losing their homes or everything they possessed—they had stopped getting rich quick. That was all. And I thought, our profoundest emotions should be reserved for real things—human beings, people we love—not digits on the stock exchange.

We live in a money culture—no doubt about that. Think of a successful person; conjure one up in your mind right now. It may be you; it may be someone you know or a celebrity. How do you judge that person as successful? What immediately springs to mind? Is it that they have a great relationship? That their kids are happy? Is it that everybody likes them, or that they really like their job? Or do you think of the money they earn, of the kind of place they live in, of the sports vehicle and the two-seater in the driveway? These private judgments are in scale with a general public feeling that if our economy is in good shape, our world is in good shape. And governments are praised not by their health and education provision, or their welfare record, or by employment or foreign policy, but by the robustness—or not—of the central economy. Capitalism says that society must become richer and richer, that whatever the cost, economies must grow. Once we subscribe to money as the core value, what follows is a deregulated, twenty-four-hour society, where the right to sleep, the right to peace and quiet, the right to family life, the right to human-friendly work patterns and human-friendly hours all become far less important than the right to make money.

Against this golden calf in the wilderness, where everybody comes to buy and sell, art offers a different rate of exchange. The artist does not turn time into money; the artist—whether writer, painter, musician—turns time into energy, time into intensity, time into vision. And the exchange that art offers is an exchange in kind—of energy for energy, intensity for intensity, vision for vision. Can we make the return? Do we want to? When people complain that art is hard work, they really mean that our increasingly passive entertainments do not equip us for the demands that art makes. Art is not a passive activity. We have to get involved. Imagination always means involvement, and as soon as your mind is open to a different level of seeing, thinking, hearing, or understanding, you start asking questions. Money culture hates questions.

Part of the triumph of capitalism has been to make itself seem natural—not only the best way to live but also the inevitable way, the only way. Art asks questions. I don't mean directly, or politically, though that is sometimes the case. I mean that art, by its very nature, is a question. A question about who we are, about what things matter. Art stands as an eternal question mark at the end of money's confident rhetoric. This is partly because artists themselves cannot work in the way a money culture demands—that is, to order, and with guaranteed results in a specified time—and partly because art just can't be controlled. It doesn't fit in with any economic models. It can't be predicted. It can't be done away with or phased out or put on growth hormones. So either we ignore it and say it's not essential, not important—might have been once, but isn't now—or we indulge it and see it as a kind of charming charity, a sort of ornament to life in the way that ladies were once ornaments to gentlemen.

But art is not an ornament, or a charity, or a waste of time. It is a completely different way of looking at the world. At the core of art is an intensity of experience totally lacking from a money culture, whose purpose is to dilute every other value to below the value of itself. Art wants you to concentrate; money wants you to dissipate. Far from being about hard work, a money culture is about incredible waste of effort, as people labor for no other purpose than to make more of the same: money. The only thing money won't let you dissipate is itself. You can waste your life, but money has to be saved—because money is precious, and life is not.

But what can art do for us, in a world of corporate culture? Isn't it just temporary relief, or escapism? When I sit down to read a book without interruption or to listen to a piece of music at home or at the concert hall, without interruption, or to look at a painting, without interruption, the first thing I'm doing is turning my gaze inward. The outside world, with all its demands and distractions, has to wait—not something it likes doing. As I turn my attention away from the world, I draw my energy away from the world. I'm not passive, but I'm in a state of alert rest, where the artwork can reach me with its own energies, very different energies to the getting and spending going on all around me. The creativity and concentration put into the making of the artwork begins to cross-current into me. It's not simply about being recharged, as in a good night's sleep or a vacation; it's about being charged at a different voltage. When I read Emily Dickinson or William Carlos Williams, I'm not just reading a poet's take on the world—I am entering into a completely different world, and I don't mean a fantasy screen. I mean a world built from the beginning on different principles. William Carlos Williams wrote, "It is difficult / to get the news from poems / yet men die miserably every day / for lack / of what is found there."

Art's counterculture, however diverse, holds in plain sight what a material world denies: love and imagination. Art is made out of a passionate, reckless love of the work in its own right, as though nothing else exists, and an imaginative force that creates something new out of disparate material. Art's experiments are not funded by huge state programs, venture capital, or junk bonds. They're done when one person picks up a pen or brush, or sits down at the piano, or takes a piece of clay and changes it forever. Art is about the individual, the individual commitment not tethered to reward. For the maker, and later the reader or the viewer or the listener, there is no obvious reward. There is only the thing-in-itself, because you want it, because you're drawn to it. It speaks to the part of us that is fully human, the part that belongs only to ourselves, not mechanized, socialized, pacified, integrated, but voice-to-voice, across time, singing a song pitched to the human ear, singing of destiny, of fear, of loss, of hope, of renewal, of change, of connection, of all the subtle and fragile relationships between men and women, their children, their country, and all the things not measured or understood by the census figures and the gross national product. Art slips through, and us with it—slips past the border police and the currency controls, to talk as we've always wanted to, about matters of the spirit and the heart, to imagine a world not dominated by numbers, to find in colors and poetry and sand an equivalence to our deepest feelings, a language for what we are.

What are we?

Human beings, made of flesh, with something strange called the *soul* that just won't let us forget about the invisible worlds we deny. Art is the soul's ally and calls us out, past what we know and take for granted, into what we dream. This is the balance we need, the balance the material world can't give us.

I want to go further now. How do we learn? All animals, human and not, learn by copying. My kitten goes out the cat door because she sees my cat do it. My godchild sits with a book, usually upside down, because she sees me sitting with a book, hopefully the right way up. It's a good method, and it works. Humans also learn by analogy. We explain things to children by saying, "It's like this," or "It's like that." And we explain the world to ourselves in much the same way. When anything new comes along, we refer it to what we already know. Our brain finds a template and uses it to formulate the new experience or emotion. This is our evolutionary inheritance.

We could say that education begins where evolution ends, because it is the purpose of education (or should be) to provide us with as many templates as possible to use in interpreting what goes on around us and inside us. The more templates we have, the better adapted and adjusted we can be. Indeed, one of the old-fashioned arguments for a liberal education was that too much specialism is bad for people; it narrows our range, not only in the sense of what we know but also, more crucially, in how we can interpret what we know. In a world as complex as ours, we need all the templates we can get.

So many people are frightened and unsettled by the world we live in because they have no real way of understanding it. They have to take it on trust, believe what they hear, stand aside as spectators. Business studies, life sciences, computing technology, MBAs, all the fashionable industry-led courses may tell us how to make money, but they don't tell us anything about human beings. And I don't mean you should enroll for a night class in human resources management or whatever is the current fad. The fact is that human beings are what we have to deal with, including ourselves, and human nature always has been, and always will be, the raw material of art. That is why time spent reading books, looking at pictures, or listening to music is never a waste of time. What you find there are templates that make sense of yourself, and yourself in the world.

All right. But there's more to it than that. When we engage with a fully achieved work of art and go past what it can tell us into what it is, we are confronted by the kind of new experience that our brain doesn't like. Remember, the brain will try to explain everything by what it knows already. Give it something new, and I mean *really* new, and it has to reconfigure itself—the hippocampus actually alters its chemical makeup. Art challenges the "I" that we are and asks us to see beyond our own assumptions, prejudices, and templates. When we force that brain of ours to reconfigure itself, we're claiming a little bit more light, a little bit more land. In true evolutionary terms, we are expanding our territory, and what was good for the savannah isn't good for the plain. We shake ourselves up. Or maybe we *wake* ourselves up, for art is a very good alarm clock.

Art won't let you sleepwalk from one experience to another, going through the motions of life. Art keeps you alert, not in the hyper, super-exhausted state of video games and too much TV, but alert to life, its beauty, and its complexity. By demanding from us, art returns to us what we really need—above all, that element of surprise, the kind of unexpected delight we enjoy so much in children. When we learn to look at things—and painting shows us how to do that—we look at everything in the world with new eyes. And when we learn to listen—and music teaches us how to do that—we start to hear the tones and the melodies of everyday existence. When we understand the rhythms of poetry and the images of language, we begin to hear the language of what is around us. The life of things.

The work of the artist is to see into the life of things, I suppose what the scientist Rupert Sheldrake would call "morphic resonance"—the inner life of the thing that cannot be explained away biologically, chemically, or physically. I'd call it "imaginative reality." The reality of the imagination leaves nothing out. It is the most complete reality we can know. The artist is physical; and it is in the work of true artists, in whatever medium, that we find the most moving and poignant studies of the world that we can touch and feel, whether human or natural. When Cezanne paints an apple or a tree, he doesn't paint a copy of an apple or a tree, he paints its reality, the whole that it is, the whole that is lost to us as we walk past it, eat it, chop it down. It's through the artist, who lives more intensely than the rest of us, that we can rediscover the intensity of the physical world.

But not only the physical world. The earth is not flat, and neither is reality. Reality is continuous, multiple, simultaneous, complex, abundant, and partly invisible. The imagination alone can fathom this, because the imagination is not limited by the world of sense experience. It's not necessary to be shut up in oneself, to grind through life like an ox at a mill. Human beings are capable of powered flight. Our dreams of outer space are only a reflection of the inner space we could occupy if we knew how. Art knows how. At the same time as art is prizing away old, dead structures that have rusted, almost unnoticed, into our flesh, art is pushing at the boundaries we thought were fixed. The only boundaries are the boundaries of our imagination. We need art to remind us of that.

Years ago, when I was hiding books under my mattress or learning long passages from them in the library, the most liberating and the most painful side to it all was the emotion evoked. My early life was so harsh that one way round it would have been not to feel at all. It's a common response, and an understandable one. When things are too much, we shut down. We damage ourselves to save ourselves. We hope feeling will come back later. But very often, it doesn't. If it does, we fear it. We've been hurt before. We don't want to be hurt again.

In the economy of the body, the limbic highway that governs the emotions is given right-of-way over the neural system that runs the intellect. That is why, at moments of panic or deep stress, even the most controlled of us acts instinctively. It is also why so much of what we think of as Western civilization is about controlling emotion. We value rationality over instinct, logic over feeling; we say the head must rule the heart. There's good in this, because civilization is artificial—it isn't tribal or instinctive. It's a social and moral code that depends on conscious effort. The only way large numbers of people can live together is by being able to control themselves as individuals, to negotiate, to reason, often to ignore what we feel, and to look through the pressing emotional content of a situation into the long-term consequences. And yet, the split between heart and head isn't helpful or healing. Is there an answer?

Is there a way of letting emotion through, without emotion overwhelming us? I'll risk it, and I'll say that art has always been the answer. Why? Because art shows us how to end the war, the war between heart and head, the war between reason and emotion. An achieved work of art combines an extraordinary hardiness of form with an exquisite emotional sense. Its toughness lets it contain emotion without suppressing or damaging it. Feeling breathes through form.

In an age of mechanization, digitalization, mass production, and mass values, art is a hand-cut path through the layers of resistance and fear that protect us from feeling. In front of a picture, or in the pages of a book, or listening to a piece of music, I find the feelings I need to feel but within the structure I need to feel safe.

Why do we need to feel?

I have noticed that failure of feeling is accompanied by a desire for ever more violent sensations. We *have* to feel; and if we cannot feel richly, then we'll feel crudely. The violence in our society, the emphasis on sex, the spectator tragedies of the kind that TV and media adore, measure the weakness of our emotional range. For too many people, feeling is calibrated to the soap opera values of popular culture. This reduces both strength and type of feeling to something like a pair of hot and cold faucets. It is odd that, while we agree that billions of dollars must be spent to unravel even the simplest workings of genetic code, the workings of our hearts can safely be left to the maunderings of a cheap sitcom. We value sensitive machines; money is always available to make them more sensitive yet, so that they detect minerals deep in the earth's crust—radioactivity thousands of miles away. We don't value sensitive human beings, and we spend no money on their priority. As machines become more delicate, and human beings coarser, will antennae and fiber-optics claim for themselves what was once uniquely human? I'm not talking about rationality and logic— machines can do that. I'm talking about the strange network of fragile perceptions that means I can imagine, that teaches me to love, that shows me through recognition and tenderness the essential beat that rhythms life.

The artist as radar can help me—the artist who combines an exceptional sensibility with an exceptional control. This equipment—unfunded, unregarded, and kept tuned to untapped frequencies—will bring home signals otherwise lost to me. While NASA tracks the heavens, who will track my heart?

The American poet Muriel Rukeyser said, "What would happen if one woman told the truth about herself? / The world would split open." Art tells this truth, and it is an emotional truth. That makes it desperately needed, and desperately feared. But I know of no better communicator for our deepest feelings than art, and no better way of connecting those limbic and neural pathways that God or nature gave us to struggle with until the end of time.

Time is not ended yet, and there will be no end to the question "What is art for?" perhaps because we never stop asking the question "What are *we* for?"

We are restless, searching creatures—poignant in our smallness, triumphant in our determination not to be small. It is all these things—our determination, our aspiration, perhaps our inevitable failure—that art relays back to us. But art is more than a recording angel. It is the creative force that marks out our humanness, the creative force that seeks to bind together all the separations that we are.

CONTRIBUTORS

CHIMAMANDA NGOZI ADICHIE was born in Nigeria. She is the author of *Half of a Yellow Sun*, which won the Orange Prize and was a finalist for the National Book Critics Circle Award, and *Purple Hibiscus*, which won the Commonwealth Writers' Prize and the Hurston/Wright Legacy Award. *The Thing Around Your Neck*, her collection of stories, was short-listed for the Commonwealth Writers' Prize for Best Book in Africa. The recipient of a MacArthur Foundation Fellowship, she was named by the *New Yorker* as one of the twenty most important fiction writers today under forty years old. Her most recent novel, *Americanah*, won the National Book Critics Circle Award in Fiction and the Heartland Prize, and was named one of the *New York Times Book Review*'s Ten Best Books of the Year.

MARGARET ATWOOD is the author of more than forty books of fiction, poetry, and critical essays. Her newest novel, *MaddAddam* (2013), is the follow-up to *The Year of the Flood* (2009) and her Giller

Prize winner, *Oryx and Crake* (2009). Other recent publications include *The Door*, a volume of poetry (2007), *Payback: Debt and the Shadow Side of Wealth* (2008), and *In Other Worlds: SF and the Human Imagination* (2011). Additional titles include the 2000 Booker Prize–winning *The Blind Assassin*, *Alias Grace*, which won the Giller Prize in Canada and the Premio Mondello in Italy, *The Robber Bride*, *Cat's Eye*, *The Handmaid's Tale*, and *The Penelopiad*. Atwood lives in Toronto with the writer Graeme Gibson.

RUSSELL BANKS is the prize-winning author of seventeen books of fiction, including the novels *Continental Drift* and *Cloudsplitter*, both finalists for the Pulitzer Prize. Two of his novels, *Affliction* and *The Sweet Hereafter*, have been made into critically acclaimed, prize-winning films. He has published six collections of short stories, most recently *A Permanent Member of the Family*. His work is widely translated, and in 2010 he was made an Officier de l'Ordre des Arts et des Lettres by the Minister of Culture of France. He is the former president of the International Parliament of Writers and a member of the American Academy of Arts and Letters. He was the New York State Author, 2004–2008, and in 2014 was inducted into the New York Writers Hall of Fame. He resides in upstate New York and Miami Beach, Florida.

E. L. DOCTOROW's work has been published in thirty-two languages. His novels include *Andrew's Brain*, *The March*, *City of God*, *Welcome to Hard Times*, *The Book of Daniel*, *Ragtime*, *Loon Lake*, *World's Fair*, *Billy Bathgate*, *The Waterworks*, and *Homer and Langley*. He has published three volumes of short fiction, *Lives of the Poets*, *Sweet Land Stories*, and *All the Time in the World*, and three collections of essays, *Creationists*, *Reporting the Universe* (The Harvard-Massey Lectures in the History of American Civilization), and *Jack London, Hemingway, and the Constitution.* There have been five film adaptations of his work. Among his honors are the National Book Award, two PEN/Faulkner Awards, three National Book Critics Circle Awards, the PEN/Saul Bellow Award for Achievement in American Fiction, the Gold Medal for Fiction of the American Academy of Arts and Letters, and the presidentially conferred National Humanities Medal.

EDWARD P. JONES was born in Washington, DC, in 1950. He attended the local public schools and won a scholarship to Holy Cross College. Seven years after he graduated from college, he earned his MFA at the University of Virginia. After a series of jobs, he began working for a tax newsletter, first as a proofreader and then eventually as a columnist, a position he held for more than ten years. During this time Jones kept on writing. His first short story was published in *Essence* in 1976. Since then he has had stories published in the *New Yorker*, the *Paris Review*, *Ploughshares*, and *Callaloo*. He has taught creative writing at the University of Virginia, George Mason University, the University of Maryland, and Princeton University. Jones's first collection of short stories, *Lost in the City*, was published in 1992 and won the PEN/Hemingway Award; it was short-listed for the National Book Award, and was the recipient of a Lannan Foundation Award. His first novel, *The Known World* (2003), received the 2004 Pulitzer Prize for Fiction, and he was named a MacArthur Fellow for 2004. *All Aunt Hagar's Children*, his latest collection of short stories, was published in 2006.

URSULA KROEBER LE GUIN was born in 1929 in Berkeley, California, and lives in Portland, Oregon. As of 2014, she has published twenty-one novels, eleven volumes of short stories, four collections of essays, twelve books for children, six volumes of poetry, and four of translation, and has received many honors and awards, including the Hugo, Nebula, National Book, and PEN/ Malamud awards. Her most recent publications are *Finding My Elegy (New and Selected Poems, 1960–2010)* and *The Unreal and the Real (Selected Short Stories)*, which received the 2012 Oregon Book Award for Fiction.

MARILYNNE ROBINSON is the author of *Gilead*, which won the 2005 Pulitzer Prize for Fiction and the 2004 National Book Critics Circle Award for Fiction. Her most recent novel, *Home*, a companion to *Gilead*, won the 2008 Los Angeles Times Book Prize for Fiction and the 2009 Orange Prize for Fiction. Robinson is also the author of the modern classic *Housekeeping* (available in paperback from Picador), which won the PEN/Ernest Hemingway Award for First Fiction and the Richard and Hinda Rosenthal Award from the Academy of American Arts and Letters and was nominated for the Pulitzer Prize. Robinson received a Lila Wallace-Reader's Digest Writer's Award in 1990 and the prestigious Mildred and Harold Strauss Living Award from the American Academy of Arts and Letters in 1998. A new novel, *Lila*, is forthcoming (2014) from Farrar, Straus and Giroux. She is also the author of four books of nonfiction, *Mother Country*, *The Death of Adam*, *Absence of Mind*, and *When I Was a Child I Read Books*. In 2013 President Obama awarded her the National Humanities Medal. Dr. Robinson teaches at the University of Iowa Writers' Workshop.

WALLACE STEGNER wrote thirty-five books over a sixty-year career. Among the novels are *The Big Rock Candy Mountain* (1943), *Joe Hill* (1950), *All the Little Live Things* (Commonwealth Club Gold Medal, 1967), *Angle of Repose* (Pulitzer Prize, 1972), *The Spectator Bird* (National Book Award, 1977), *Recapitulation*

(1979), *Collected Stories* (1990), and *Crossing to Safety* (1987). His nonfiction includes *Beyond the Hundredth Meridian* (1954), *Wolf Willow (A History, a Story, and a Memory of the Last Plains Frontier)* (1962), *The Sound of Mountain Water* (1969), and *Where the Bluebird Sings to the Lemonade Springs: Living and Writing in the West* (1992), which earned him a nomination for the National Book Critics Circle Award. In 1946 Stegner started the Creative Writing Program at Stanford University, where he served on the faculty until 1971. He also taught at the University of Utah, the University of Wisconsin, and Harvard University. His students include Wendell Berry, Larry McMurtry, Ernest Gaines, Raymond Carver, Edward Abbey, and Poet Laureate of the United States Robert Hass. Stegner has twice been a Guggenheim Fellow and a Senior Fellow of the National Endowment for the Humanities. He was a member of the National Academy of Arts and Sciences and of the National Academy of Arts and Letters. He died at eighty-four, on April 13, 1993.

ROBERT STONE's novel *Dog Soldiers* (1974) won the National Book Award. His other novels include *A Flag for Sunrise* (1981), which was nominated for the PEN/Faulkner Award, *Children of Light* (1986), and Bay of Souls (2003). He also published a memoir, *Prime Green: Remembering the Sixties*, in 2007. His latest novel, *Death of the Black-Haired Girl*, was published in fall of 2013. He lives in Key West, Florida.

JEANETTE WINTERSON OBE is a British writer of fiction, screenplays, essays, and journalism. She has won many awards, including the E. M. Forster Award from the American Academy of Arts and Letters. Her best-selling memoir, *Why Be Happy When You Could Be Normal*, was published in the States by Grove Press.

ACKNOWLEDGMENTS

Tin House Books and Literary Arts would like to thank the following individuals:

Lee Montgomery, for the original vision of celebrating Literary Arts' anniversary in this way.

Molly Reid and Mona Moraru, for listening to audio files and taking excellent notes.

Curtis Moore, for additional proofreading eyes.

Literary Arts staff members Susan Denning and Mel Wells; previous directors Julie Mancini, Carrie Hoops, and Elizabeth Burnett; and board member Jon Raymond.

We would also like to thank all of the subscribers, audience members, and authors who have been part of the Portland Arts and Lectures series over the past thirty years.

▌Literary Arts

"Literary Arts is one of the indispensable literary centers in the country."

— SALMAN RUSHDIE

S ince 1984, Literary Arts has built community around literature. Through live literary events, awards, fellowships, and creative writing classes and seminars for teens and adults, we strive to foster connections throughout our state, and between the larger literary world and Oregon. Our mission is to engage readers, support writers, and inspire the next generation with great literature.

OUR PROGRAMS:

Portland Arts & Lectures brings the world's most celebrated writers, artists, and thinkers to Oregon to engage with our community

Oregon Book Awards & Fellowships supports, promotes, and celebrates Oregon's writers and publishers.

Writers in the Schools inspires public high school students to write, revise, edit, publish, and perform their own creative writing.

Delve Readers Seminars engages readers in exploring challenging books in lively discussion-based seminars led by an experienced scholar.

Literary Arts is a community-based nonprofit literary center located in downtown Portland, with a 30-year history of serving Oregon's readers and writers. To support Literary Arts visit: www.literary-arts.org.

"Literary Arts plays an essential role in the thriving literary community in Oregon and it's so important that their work continues."

— CHERYL STRAYED, Oregon Book Award winner (*Wild*)